76

99BB

COMMUNICATION AND AFFECT

A Comparative Approach

CONTRIBUTORS

URSULA BELLUGI

D. E. BERLYNE

VICTOR J. DE GHETT

JACOB L. GEWIRTZ

HARRY F. HARLOW

MARGARET K. HARLOW

EDWARD S. KLIMA

DAVID PREMACK

J. P. SCOTT

IRWIN M. SPIGEL

Communication and Affect

A COMPARATIVE APPROACH

Edited by

THOMAS ALLOWAY   LESTER KRAMES

PATRICIA PLINER

Erindale College
University of Toronto
Clarkson, Ontario, Canada

ACADEMIC PRESS   *New York and London*   *1972*

ACADEMIC PRESS, INC.
111 Fifth Avenue, New York, New York 10003

United Kingdom Edition published by
ACADEMIC PRESS, INC. (LONDON) LTD.
24/28 Oval Road, London NW1

LIBRARY OF CONGRESS CATALOG CARD NUMBER: 72-7683

PRINTED IN THE UNITED STATES OF AMERICA

CONTENTS

List of Contributors   vii
Foreword   ix
Preface   xi
Acknowledgments   xiii

The Language of Love   1

Harry F. Harlow and Margaret K. Harlow

The Language of Basic Trust   4
The Language of Play   9
The Language of Lust   12
Summary   18
References   18

Attachment and Dependence: Some Strategies and Tactics in the Selection and Use of Indices for Those Concepts   19

Jacob L. Gewirtz

Introduction   19
Some Frequently Employed Indices of Attachment or Dependence   24
Assumptions Often Underlying the Use of Attachment and Dependence Indices   30
Some Considerations Regarding the Number and Types of Indices to Employ   34
The Empirical Literature and Attachment-Dependence Indices   39
Recapitulation   42
References   44

Two Problems in Cognition: Symbolization, and From Icon to Phoneme   51

David Premack

Symbolization: More Primitive Than Language   51
From Icon to Phoneme   58
References   65

The Signs of Language in Child and Chimpanzee   67

Edward S. Klima and Ursula Bellugi

The Signs of Language   67
Structure and Well Formedness   70
Language Experiments with Chimpanzees   74
Language in a Different Mode   77
The Sign Itself   79
Preliminary Experimental Data: Memory Tests   90
Observations on Sign as a First Language   91
References   96

Affective Aspects of Aesthetic Communication   97

D. E. Berlyne

Experiments with Visual Patterns   102
Experiments with Single Sounds   104
Experiments with Sound Sequences   106
Interestingness, Pleasingness, and Exploration   110
Experiments on Affective Responses to Poetry   111
Conclusions   116
References   117

The Communication of Affect and the Possibility of
Man—Machine as a New Dyad   119

Irwin M. Spigel

Experiment 1   120
Experiment 2   126
References   128

Development of Affect in Dogs and Rodents   129

J. P. Scott and Victor J. De Ghett

Introduction   129
Development of Distress Vocalization in the Dog   130
Development of Affect in Infant Rodents   138
Discussion   144
References   148

Author Index   151
Subject Index   154

LIST OF CONTRIBUTORS

Numbers in parentheses indicate the pages on which the authors' contributions begin.

URSULA BELLUGI (67), The Salk Institute for Biological Studies, San Diego, California

D. E. BERLYNE (97), Department of Psychology, University of Toronto, Toronto, Canada

VICTOR J. DE GHETT* (129), Department of Psychology, Bowling Green State University, Bowling Green, Ohio

JACOB L. GEWIRTZ (19), National Institute of Mental Health, Bethesda, Maryland

HARRY F. HARLOW (1), University of Wisconsin, Madison, Wisconsin

MARGARET K. HARLOW† (1), University of Wisconsin, Madison, Wisconsin

EDWARD S. KLIMA (67), Department of Linguistics, University of California at San Diego, La Jolla, California

DAVID PREMACK (51), Department of Psychology, University of California, Santa Barbara, California

J. P. SCOTT (129), Department of Psychology, Bowling Green State University, Bowling Green, Ohio

IRWIN M. SPIGEL (119), Department of Psychology, Erindale College, University of Toronto, Toronto, Canada

*Present address: Department of Psychology, State University of New York, Potsdam, New York.

† Deceased.

vii

FOREWORD

Erindale College, the newest of the University of Toronto's eight undergraduate colleges, opened in the fall of 1967 on its own campus 25 miles west of the University's main campus in the heart of the city. The College opened in small preliminary facilities. From the outset, plans were laid for the development of extensive research and teaching laboratory facilities which would serve the needs of Erindale's faculty and students. Included in these plans was the development of psychological laboratories designed the meet the needs of those members of the University's department of psychology who are located on the Erindale Campus. The papers which appear in this book were originally delivered at a Symposium on Communication and Affect, which was held to celebrate the opening of the first group of psychology laboratories at Erindale.

There were two major forces which shaped the selection of the theme for this Symposium. On the one hand, we wanted a theme which was in keeping with Erindale College's interest in interdisciplinary studies, particularly communication. On the other hand, we wanted to select a theme that would engage the interest of the broader university, psychological, and scientific communities. Accordingly, Communication and Affect was chosen.

PREFACE

At an intuitive level, men have long believed that the communication of affective or emotional feelings was one of the most important and rewarding aspects of the human experience. However, at the present time in our history, it appears that we may be approaching a crisis in affective communication produced by the growing difficulties which individuals face in establishing meaningful interpersonal relationships in an increasingly impersonal society. This crisis is reflected in the construction of a rhetoric and philosophy of alienation, in frequent criticisms of our educational and political institutions as resembling assembly-line factories and in the alleged decline of the family as an institution in which meaningful interpersonal interactions occur. In response, many new techniques for achieving close interpersonal relationships are being tried. Among these are the wide-ranging reforms which are being introduced in educational and religious institutions and experimentation with various nontraditional life style and communal forms of living. Moreover, friendship in the form of psychotherapy and encounter groups is becoming an increasingly saleable commodity in our society.

Unfortunately, little empirical evidence exists concerning the causes, functions, and dysfunctions of human affective communication; and many of those involved in seeking to overcome the problems which we have outlined appear to believe that science and social science have little to offer, even potentially, to the solution process. We disagree. Hence, we decided to initiate a series of symposia which would attempt to aid in providing a framework or starting point for a scientific approach to these problems. To this end, we have called upon eminent scientists in related areas to provide papers which could serve as resource material for those interested in communication and affect. We hope that the empirical findings and theoretical statements contained in these papers will play a seminal role in stimulating future empirical research and thinking in this area.

In the present volume, we have approached affect and communication from a broad phylogenetic and ontogenetic perspective. Accordingly, the papers deal with a wide variety of affective responses and with communication between man and man, man and machine, man and chimpanzee, monkey and monkey, dog and dog, and rodent and rodent.

For example, Harry and Margaret Harlow deal with sex differences in the development of affective relationships in rhesus monkeys, while Jacob Gewirtz advances valuable methodological and theoretical guidelines for research on behavioral development generally. David Premack, and Ursula Bellugi and Edward Klima discuss the development of proficiency in the use of language-like symbolic systems in the young chimpanzee and in the deaf human child, while John Scott and Victor DeGhett discuss the development of nonlinguistic affective communication in young rodents and dogs. Finally, Daniel Berlyne and Irwin Spigel describe the affective response of young human adults to aesthetic stimuli and machines, respectively.

This volume thus contains a wide variety of basic research findings and theoretical orientations which should be of use to psychologists, linguists, and educators interested in the evolution and development of communication and affect in mammals.

ACKNOWLEDGMENTS

We would like to take this opportunity to thank the many people whose support and encouragement contributed to the success of the symposium. It is necessary to thank Professor I. M. Spigel, Associate Dean of Erindale College, who first suggested the idea of holding a symposium. Professor J. Tuzo Wilson and Professor E. A. Robinson, Principal and Dean, respectively, of Erindale College arranged for the necessary financial support. Professors Wilson and Robinson, along with Professors G. E. Macdonald and Daniel E. Berlyne provided invaluable advice and enthusiasm which helped to make the Symposium a reality. We would be remiss if we did not acknowledge the dedicated assistance of the College's nonacademic staff under the direction of Mr. A. Boorman, Mr. A. Miller, Mrs. G. Anderson, and Mr. S. Wardle. In addition, Mrs. Doris Heckman, our harassed secretary, provided a semblance of organization which would otherwise have been missing.

Finally, although their remarks do not appear in this volume, the discussants of the major papers made an important contribution to the Symposium. Accordingly, we would like to thank Professors G. E. Finley, J. E. Grusec, J. A. Hogan, G. E. Macdonald, and P. P. M. Meincke of the University of Toronto, Professor W. R. Thompson of Queen's University, and Dr. V. M. Rakoff of the Clarke Institute of Psychiatry.

THE LANGUAGE OF LOVE[1]

Harry F. Harlow   *Margaret K. Harlow*[2]

Department of Psychology
University of Wisconsin
Madison, Wisconsin

For over a decade we have studied the mechanisms by which monkeys reach normal social and sexual development. These mechanisms are the maturation and integration of the various affectional systems – mother love, infant love, age-mate or peer love, heterosexual love, and paternal love. Since all kinds of love, by our definition, involve social relationships, their normal development can be achieved only by the action and interaction of complex channels of communication.

A number of studies have shown that rhesus monkeys are capable of responding to emotional states of other monkeys on the basis of relatively subtle visual and auditory cues (Sackett, 1966), and monkeys doubtless make use of these capabilities in the course of their daily incursions and excursions. It is almost equally certain that human ethologists will eventually designate and describe all of these subtle communications which transmit useful information.

Fortunately for the disturbed or distraught man who is unwilling or unable to devote all his life to ethology, the information essential to the evolution and existence of a species is frequently transmitted from one species member to another by techniques which are far from subtle. Thus, we shall describe in large part the social behaviors that result from social information, whether or not the exact nature of that information can always be precisely defined.

We shall consider the kinds of information that must be socially received for

[1] This research was supported by USPHS grants MH-11894 and RR-0167 from the National Institutes of Health to the University of Wisconsin Primate Laboratory and Regional Primate Research Center, respectively.
[2] Deceased.

1

the maintenance or development of representative monkey affectional systems. Because affection and love are not always subtle, it is not surprising that the language of love can usually be translated or inferred without recourse to behavioral nuances and niceties of communication.

From the point of view of social–sexual development we believe that mother love and peer love are the all-important affectional systems. We will have something to say about the former and considerable to say about the latter subsequently. Although we are impressed by mother love and believe that it is here to stay, we shall place immediate emphasis on the closely related infant love-affectional system, the love of the infant for the mother. We take this viewpoint because we know little about the informational channels that cause the mother to lavish love on the infant and much more about the informational channels that cause the infant to lavish love on the mother.

Although auditory and visual communication channels play an important role in the formation and an enormous role in the maintenance of the affectional responses that bind the infant monkey to the mother, the basic early information is transmitted by way of cutaneous and proprioceptive channels. Some years ago we demonstrated this fact by simultaneously comparing the responsiveness of neonatal monkeys to two inanimate surrogate mothers – a terrycloth mother and a wire mother, either one of which could be denied or endowed at will with lactational capabilities. The data showed that the infants had an enormous preference for the cloth surrogate and that nursing was a variable of little importance, conceivably of no importance. Of course, we presumed that the information transmitted through contactual and propriocep-tive channels provided the primary variables releasing the infant's love or love responses for the mother. This presumption was correct if judgment was made on the basis of our single initial test situation. However, subsequent research revealed an enormous complexity and multiplicity of variables involved in the infant's attachment to the mother.

In a subsequent study Furchner and Harlow (1969) rated the relevant efficiency of various surrogate surfaces in releasing infant attachment and obtained a preferential ordering from wool to rayon to nylon to sandpaper. We know that spun nylon and cheesecloth effectively impart contact comfort, but we do not know whether sandpaper is less preferred than wire. Furthermore, wire is not an aversive or painful contact surface, but merely one at or near the bottom of the contact comfort totem pole. Perhaps it strains the imagination to think of communication being transmitted from sandpaper and hardware cloth, but it is undoubtedly wrong to think of communication in any other manner. As we have indicated, the transmission of contact comfort information is a highly subtle and selective form of communication, and contact comfort is doubtless the primary variable determining the infant's love for the mother.

We believe that all important behaviors, particularly emotional behaviors, are mediated by multiple variables, and the infant's tie to the mother certainly qualifies as a complex emotional behavior. With this simple idea in mind, we redesigned and expanded our surrogate researches and were able to demonstrate the multivariate nature of infant love. In our original surrogate study we discovered that contact comfort was of overwhelming importance. This discovery was true. Our original study also failed to reveal any other variable that was of significance. This finding later proved false.

In a positive attempt to demonstrate that the breast and activities associated with the breast played a role in the formation and maintenance of the infant—mother bond, we tested the responses of infants to two cloth surrogates, one blue and one tan so that the nursing surrogate was differentially color-coded and the variable of contact comfort was held constant. Under these circumstances, the monkey infants developed an early preference for the bounteous bosom of the nursing surrogate, and this preference persisted for over 90 days. Obviously the information by which the infants chose liquid love as contrasted to liquid lack was transmitted by the color-coded visual variables and reinforced by oral activities transmitting information by way of gustatory and olfactory channels.

When disturbed or ill, human infants are soothed by gentle rocking, and this led us to conduct two experiments to determine if appropriate information transmitted through proprioceptive or vestibular channels would influence maternal choice by infant monkeys. To measure this, we constructed two surrogates that were identical in body surface, color, and lactational capabilities, and differed only in that one was stationary and the other rocked gently back and forth. We also constructed two terrycloth-covered plane surfaces. These were also identical in all characteristics except that one was stationary and the other gently rocked. The infants rather rapidly developed a preference for the moving surrogate over the stationary surrogate, and for the moving plane over the stationary plane, and these preferences continued for about 150 days.

Finally we investigated the role of maternal temperature variables by creating various "hot" and "cold" mother surrogates. In the first study, we allowed infants to choose between a room-temperature cloth surrogate and a wire surrogate warmed by a heating coil inserted within its wire body, which actually raised the temperature of the heated surrogate about 10°F. Warmth proved to be a variable of such importance that, throughout the first 15 days of life, neonatal monkeys actually preferred the heated wire surrogate to the unheated cloth surrogate. This is the only maternal condition we have ever encountered in which a secondary variable transmitted information of such importance to infant monkeys that they preferred wire mothers to cloth mothers. Actually, it should be noted that this preference was shortly reversed, and the cloth mother assumed her expected mother role.

The variable of modest maternal temperature elevation yielded the dramatic results just described, but these results were actually less profound and less protracted than those achieved by the use of surrogates with ice-cold veins. Baby monkeys raised from birth on a cold surrogate whose body temperature was less than $10°F$ below room temperature developed a strong and persistent aversion to this frigid female fiend, and retreated from her as far as possible, while gazing at her with no thought or feeling of friendship.

The Language of Basic Trust

We had long known that one of the primary functions of the real mother, human or monkey, was that of instilling in its infant a feeling of security or – as it has been called – basic trust (Erikson, 1950). Although we confidently expected when we began our surrogate studies that infant monkeys would like or learn to like cloth surrogate mothers, particularly cloth surrogate nursing mothers, we stood in awe of the phenomenon of basic trust, firmly believing that the language variables and communication channels essential to the formation of security and basic trust transcended those that we could implant in brainless mothers, regardless of their bodily charms. Perhaps we overestimated female brains and underestimated the pervasive and persuasive charms of female bodies. During the course of our studies of the responses of infants placed with cloth surrogate mothers in a large strange test room or open field, we discovered that by approximately 80 days of age the infant monkeys had achieved a strong sense of security or basic trust from the cloth maternal presence.

In the open-field situation the infants would first closely embrace the cloth surrogate surface, and after they had rubbed an adequate quantum of mother love into their own bodies, they would leave the cloth surrogate and independently explore the wide world of wonder beyond the maternal confines. At any threat of danger the infants would hastily return to the ever-loving surrogate mother, cling and embrace her, and then again go forth to explore and manipulate the external physical world.

In the absence of the cloth surrogate mother, the response of the baby monkeys to a strange external environment was completely reversed. They either threw themselves prostrate on the floor or huddled on the floor and cried piteously. Similar distress responses are demonstrated by human babies when placed in an unfamiliar environment in the absence of their mother. Thus it is obvious that effective loving maternal ministrations do instill in infants a very considerable degree of basic security and trust in the mother's presence.

Different behavior occurred when monkey babies were placed in a strange environment in the presence of an unloved mother surrogate, and there is every reason to believe that human babies would respond in the same manner. The physical presence of this presumably unloving mother obviously provided the baby monkey no sense of security, for the infant made no effort to contact the strange surrogate. Instead, it lay hunched and prostrate on the floor, crying for succor and safety.

Some mothers or surrogate mothers impart security feelings to their infants, and other mothers do not. But without this love, there can be no security. Our data demonstrate that contact-comfort responses play an important role in the formation of basic security and trust — certainly in monkeys.

Baby monkeys that have achieved partial or complete physical independence from their mothers are motivated by curiosity to leave their mothers and explore the physical and social world about them. If the infants are frightened by any fear stimulus during these explorations, they rush back to the mother and cling tightly. We assume that the maternal information transmitted by pleasurable contact comfort acts to inhibit the infant's fear, whether this be through a process of deconditioning, extinction, or desensitization. Actually, by the time the infant has reached this stage, the mother's body or cloth surrogate body should be a much more efficacious agent for desensitization than a program of self-induced progressive relaxation.

Always, after the infant's fear abates and emotional composure is restored, the infant monkey will be lured again to explore the external environment, where it will certainly be frightened and will once more return to seek and receive maternal comfort and reassurance. After this process has been repeated many times over a period of days, weeks, or months, all frightening stimuli other than those which are truly painful or perilous will be totally extinguished or desensitized. When this state is achieved, the information provided by either the sight of or contact with the mother or the cloth surrogate will be sufficient to impart a broadly generalized basic security to the infant.

The achievement of security and basic trust through information transmitted by the maternal body surface sounds too simple to be true, and no doubt it is not completely true. There are many channels of security information provided by the real mother that are not provided by the surrogate. The real mother may go to the aid of the infant without waiting for the infant to come to her; the real mother may eliminate external fear stimuli by postural threats; and if these techniques are inadequate, the real mother may tear the intruder — at least some intruders — into shreds in her infant's presence. Such information would certainly build security and trust in an infant monkey, and such information would be communicated to the infant over visual and auditory channels.

We have now discussed the communication channels between neonatal monkeys and mothers or surrogate mothers. These channels effectively regulate the infant's biological needs of nutrition and comfort, and they even regulate, at least partly, the infant's needs of basic trust and security. However, real mothers obviously do more than surrogates in that they prepare the infants in efficient, complex manners for age-mate or peer socialization and often supervise these activities.

The surrogate mother can transmit adequate physical and social information to meet neonatal needs, but a surrogate is less able to meet the changing needs of growing infants. To meet the changing needs of the growing infant, the monkey mother alters her behavior, since she cannot alter her body.

After the infant ceases to be a neonate the maternal requirements become complex and almost contradictory. We have called this the "ambivalent maternal stage." The basic neonatal needs continue in modified form, but the contradictory functions that the mother faces are those of restraining her offspring from premature independent exploration and subsequently forceably displacing from the maternal model those infants who are reluctant to accept independent existence when it is time for them to begin an end to parental dependence and acquaint themselves with the presence and perils of interacting with age-mate peers. This process is known as anti-imprinting, and is not recognized in Bavaria. It should be noted that at this age the communication channels between child and mother are clearly bidirectional. Through their behaviors, the infants communicate their intentions to the mothers, and the mothers appraise these communications, either responding positively in terms of endearment or negatively in terms of punishment.

If one merely plots the developmental trends of maternal endearment, measured by clinging and cradling (as shown in Fig. 1), and the developmental trends of rejection and punishment, plotted in Fig. 2, it is clear from a statistical viewpoint how the mother restrains her infants until they are old enough to leave and encourages their departure when the time to substitute playmates for parents has arrived.

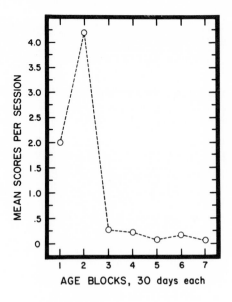

Fig. 1. Developmental course of the positive maternal responses of clasping, cradling, retrieving, and oral and manual exploration.

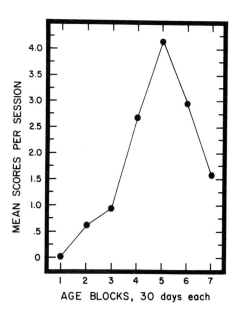

Fig. 2. Developmental course of the negative maternal responses of threatening, punishing, and avoiding.

If, as in one of our caging situations, the infant may escape through a porthole that is too small for the mother, the mother may try to lure the infant back by means of rather specific types of gestural communications. One of these is the maternal "silly grin," which is depicted in Fig. 3. To the unsophisticated human being, this may appear to be a fear response, but the infant monkey recognizes its real significance, whether or not he elects to respond appropriately to it.

Another gestural communication to lure the infant back to the mother is that of a pseudosexual present, whereby the mother approaches the infant as closely as she can and then conspicuously orients all her maternal charms toward her infant. We also call this the "hot pants" gesture. A human being, and doubtless also an adult monkey male, viewing the mother alone would ascribe a very different meaning to this gestural communication than does her infant.

All of the specific maternal responses and communications we have described so far are designed to maintain contact, or at least proximity, between the infant and the mother. None of these activities facilitates the development of age-mate affection. From the second month onward, however, monkey mothers become increasingly tolerant of the exploratory wanderings of their infants beyond the confines of maternal arms. From the third month onward they begin to transmit a qualitatively different kind of maternal information by the initiation with increasing frequency of responses of rejection and even punishment. This punishment is usually gentle, but if the infant clings too tightly or mouths the nipple too forceably the punishment can be vigorous indeed. There can be no question that these maternal activities of punishment encourage the infant,

Fig. 3. "Silly grin" by macaque mother.

which, by 3 months old, is secure in the sight of the mother as well as the clasp of the mother, to go forth on its own and explore the outside world of playthings and playmates.

Maternal punishment is only one variable producing mother-infant separation. Another major complementary variable is that of infant curiosity and object manipulation. Baby monkeys raised by real mothers or on cloth surrogate mothers show an increasing frequency of oral, manual, and visual exploratory behaviors from the first to the third month. Most observers of baby monkeys believe that curiosity is the primary force leading to mother-infant separation. Other observers believe that maternal punishment is the primary mechanism. Since all observers agree that maternal punishment and infant curiosity are the primary maternal separating mechanisms, their priority of importance is not an issue of overwhelming concern. We have always been impressed by the power of curiosity.

There are two reasons, one obvious and one far from obvious, why infants must not leave maternal protection too early in life. The obvious reason is that the tiny defenseless monkey infant alone in the natural feral habitat would be converted into a leopard luncheon or a vulture viand in a short time. Of course, the baby monkeys we raise in a civilized environment are subjected to no such needless dangers. However, there are reasons transcending lethality why infant monkeys should stay at home with their mothers until they have achieved minimal social maturity at approximately 90 days of age. If normally mothered infant monkeys are allowed to interact in small groups at about 90 days of age, they rapidly develop their full repertoire of play responses. It is absolutely essential that monkeys learn to play and learn to play effectively, since play responses form the basis for all other social behaviors, including inhibition of aggression and development of social and sexual roles.

The Language of Play

When baby-monkey pairs are placed together at 40–60 days of age, they contact each other, but do not play. Instead, they clasp each other in a viselike grip which is appropriate for the neonatal attachment to the mother, but is socially lethal when it is released and interchanged between infants. These monkeys are enormously suppressed in terms of play development (see Fig. 4). They would have been far better off had they continued maternal supervision at that stage.

If groups of four 40- to 60-day-old monkeys are permitted social interaction without maternal supervision they either huddle in a ball or enter into a dorsal–ventral chain reaction, which we have called the "choo-choo response." For these monkeys, normal interactive play may be almost entirely eliminated, and the play suppression may persist for well over half a year.

Without recourse to these data one might be led to believe that many monkey mothers are overprotective, and that the maternal overprotection delays proper monkey play and socialization and unduly denies the infants their behavioral

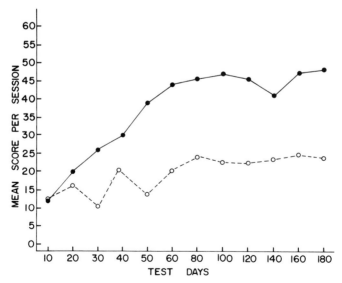

Fig. 4. Rough-and-tumble play by two together–together monkeys (o) and controls (●).

birthright. Nothing could be farther from the truth. By the time the infant monkey is old enough to play effectively with his peers, infant—mother physical bonds have usually become diluted to the extent where the infant monkey has ample time and opportunity to explore both its physical and social worlds with little or no restraint. It is far better to accept maternal restraint and enjoy effective social freedom at 120 days of age, than to escape from maternal restraint at 60 days of age and lose forever the capability for effective peer love.

The coded information activating maternal cling by an infant and that releasing reciprocal infant together—together cling is similar, if not the same. We commonly think of all social interaction as good, but the data of Fig. 4 show that the same social communication mechanism may sometimes be very beneficial and at other times, quite harmful. There is a thin line demarking what is beneficial and what could prove harmful; a single step, true or false, may determine the ultimate result.

When small groups of infant monkeys are allowed to interact at 120 days of age, they rapidly develop patterns of true play and the socially destructive patterns of reciprocal viselike cling do not appear. Furthermore, young rhesus monkeys inhibit the occurrence of the viselike cling response if they are supervised by real mothers or even by a surrogate mother. The communication channels by which surrogates inhibit infant—infant cling challenge the imagination, and even though we do not know all the parameters involved, we accept the phenomenon because it is visible.

The first socially interactive monkey play pattern to appear is that of

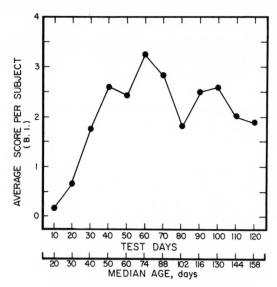

Fig. 5. Developmental course of rough-and-tumble play.

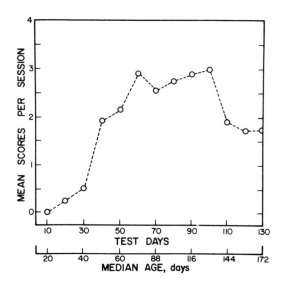

Fig. 6. Developmental course of approach–withdrawal play.

rough-and-tumble play, where the monkeys wrestle and roll and sham bite. As if by some miracle, no one ever gets hurt. The developmental course of rough-and-tumble play is graphed in Fig. 5, and it is clear that this play comes early and stays late; indeed, it does not really abate until after adolescence, when the monkeys may be saving their energies for other activities.

Somewhat later, another form of play appears. It has been given various names, such as approach–withdrawal play or contact–noncontact play. Actually it is possible that more than one play pattern is involved, such as an approach play pattern and a differentiated avoidance play pattern. The pattern as originally conceived was that of reciprocal chase, in which one monkey pursued another, but seldom made physical contact. Subsequently, the roles of the chaser and the chased would reverse. The game might continue for considerable periods of time as the monkeys moved up and down and back and forth. Furthermore, new contestants were recruited frequently and previous contestants dropped out. The developmental course of approach–withdrawal play is graphed in Fig. 6. We originally thought that approach–withdrawal play was a more complex form of play than rough-and-tumble play, and this is doubtless true. Subsequently, we had strong indications that approach–withdrawal play was predominantly feminine, whereas rough-and-tumble play was predominantly masculine. This is probably also true.

We believe that the various forms of play are the basic mechanisms underlying the age-mate or peer affectional system. During the peer stage, the monkeys learn to accept bodily contact from many more animals than in the mother love

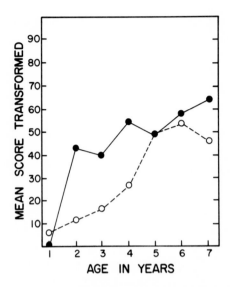

Fig. 7. Maturation of aggression in monkeys. (●) Male; (○) female.

stage, and personal security originally provided by maternal information is broadened and augmented through social support from many informational sources rather than only one. During the peer stage, the monkeys learn dominance and social ordering, and this is primarily acquired during play. Last, but certainly not least, monkeys learn social control of aggression during the peer period. Monkey aggression is a relatively late-maturing behavioral response, as shown in Fig. 7, and this is also true for human beings. The stage of age-mate love precedes the maturation of full-blown aggressive fury, and monkeys and men do not usually hate the animals, particularly the conspecific animals, that they have already learned to love. If primate hate matured before primate love, the primate order would now be long extinct.

Some monkeys become fully bloomed sexual objects during the age-mate affectional stage, but this is the exception rather than the rule. However, it is the rule, and not the exception, that monkeys denied the opportunity to develop widespread age-mate affection are bound to be losers as subsequent sexual gladiators.

The Language of Lust

We do not claim to be authorities on sexual communication by either monkeys or men, since this is a topic best left to younger men and monkeys. Memories, particularly early memories, are always vulnerable to retrospective falsification. There are enormous individual differences in monkeys concerning how and when they learn the language of love. Some female monkeys and a very few male monkeys apparently decode the language of lust, or the significance of sexual signs, early in life. This is particularly true of the monkeys raised in a rich social environment, such as our nuclear family situation (see Fig. 8), where informal communication about sex is transmitted by many monkeys of both sexes and disparate ages.

There are certain obvious requirements for the successful transmission of significant and successful sexual signs. A fundamental fact is the willingness of both the male and female to accept physical contact by a member of the opposite sex. Contactless sex warms neither the heart nor any other part of the body. Contactless love communicates only frustration. Contactless love may provide valuable information for lyrics and sonnets, but it fulfills no basic educational, creative, or procreative functions.

Giving all due credit to the importance of bodily contact acceptance, it is perfectly obvious that frenzied, frantic feel is not enough. The infant monkeys shown in Fig. 9 are rendering lip service to sexual language, and they are accepting bodily contact, but the music that emanates from their organs is eliciting neither empathy nor ecstasy from their hearts.

When mature male and female monkeys raised in total social isolation for 6 months or a year are placed together, their erotic exercises are similar in form to those of the immature monkeys already pictured. Thus, when the male approaches the female, his bodily orientation may leave much to be desired. Instead of approaching the female's posterior parts, he may grasp the side of her body and thrust laterally, as shown in Fig. 10 – a position which leaves him working at cross purposes with reality. Immature males may also grasp the female's face and engage in pelvic thrusts. We call this our head start program.

Even if the male by accident or design is properly physically oriented to the female, his efforts may come to naught. In Fig. 11 we show a female who has not responded adequately to the information the male has transmitted by close contact communication. Instead of making an attempt to stand and deliver, this female is simply sitting flat on the floor, a posture in which only her heart is in the right place. Resting in this posture, love's sweet mysteries of life will never be revealed, and the language of love will not be communicated.

Successful monkey sex requires more than the acceptance of physical contact of other monkeys, more than the feelings of friendship and companionship, and more than unlimited time to extinguish inappropriate partner responses and to reinforce appropriate partner responses. Monkey sex requires that male and female monkeys possess and release unlearned behaviors that give some support and some direction to their erotic endeavors.

The unlearned sexual responses of monkeys, or the behaviors which we believe are the unlearned sexual responses of monkeys, were first described by Rosenblum (1961), who observed infant monkeys interacting in a playroom.

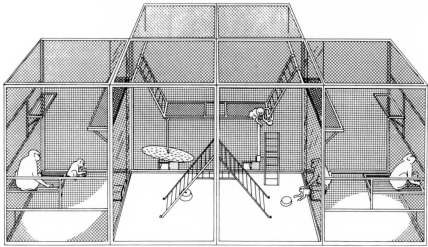

Fig. 8. Nuclear family situation.   ⌐———⌐ = 1 Foot

Fig. 9. Inadequate sexual positioning by infant monkeys.

Fig. 10. Inadequate sex by abnormal male monkey.

Fig. 11. Inadequate sexual positioning by abnormal female monkey.

These are responses far more variable than the precocious sexual fixed action patterns of the stickleback, the penguin, the pigeon, or the white rat. They are behaviors which may appear in members of either sex, but from the second month onward they show progressively greater sex differentiation until each clearly becomes a male or a female pattern. Initially they are merely sex differentiating postures; later they play a significant role in the facilitation of erotic exercises.

There is a predominantly male pattern – the threat response – and two predominantly female postures – passivity and rigidity. The threat response involves movement toward another animal, retraction of the lips, flattening of the ears, and often contact with the approached monkey's body. The differential developmental course of the threat response in male and female monkeys is shown in Fig. 12. Passivity involves turning the head and body away from an approaching monkey, and often movement away but not flight from the approaching simian.

Finally, there is the female pattern of rigidity, and its developmental course is shown in Fig. 13. When the female is approached by a male, she will turn her head away, since staring at another monkey is a threat response, and properly pious females do not threaten. Turning the head leads to bodily movement away from the approacher, and at this point the female's body stiffens. She may even look backward at the male, a movement which female monkeys often make during coitus. Early in the monkey's life, this rigidity response is not overtly sexual, but as male and female monkeys mature, rigidity in its polished form probably becomes an act of sexual elicitation and presents a posture and platform adequate to give the male moral support.

We have talked at length about the language of unlearned love, since we believe that this is an area which is commonly neglected. We have long had occasion to observe males and females that had matured beyond the free elicitation of the postures of threat, passivity, and rigidity before they had opportunities for social and sexual congress. We have been disenchanted at the resolutions of sexual postural problems by blind techniques of trial and error on the parts of these aged, amorous amateurs. Surely evolution did not leave intromission to chance.

The postures of threat, passivity, and rigidity are clearly sex-differentiating by 4 or 5 months, and although sex behavior in most rhesus monkeys is both infrequent and inept by a year of age, there is ample time to modify or adapt the sex-differentiating postures through experience by frequent feminine friendship and by meaningful masculine manipulations. Furthermore, it appears that this has been achieved to a considerable extent at a year of age. The occurrence of sexual responses by year-old male monkeys is very infrequent, but the male's infrequent sexual sorties are almost totally masculine in form. Clearly some mysterious channel of communication informed the young male along these lines. In addition, this picture of desultory dalliance is also true for the female

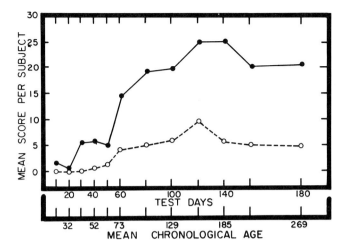

Fig. 12. Developmental course of monkey threat response. (●) Male; (○) female.

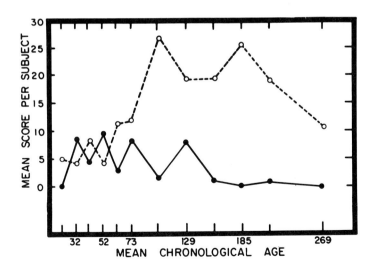

Fig. 13. Developmental course of rigidity response. (●) Male; (○) female.

macaque. Her sporadic sex is appropriate to that of a lady, or perhaps we should say her sporadic sex is appropriate to that of her body. Her occasional libidinal lessons may not be gaudy, but they are not gay.

Summary

We have now traced the development of primate love throughout its entire sequential course — from the mother—infant stage of pious, proper propinquity, throughout the adult stage of seasoned, salacious, seductive success.

In all the stages of love, much of the essential social information is supplied by unlearned communications which are, of course, rapidly overlaid by a veneer of learning. This fact has been demonstrated in monkeys because the people who study monkeys are scientists. This fact will probably never be discovered in human beings. Even if this truth is discovered in man it will never be printed in elementary psychology textbooks. Most psychology textbooks never mention love. If love is mentioned, it is defined as stimulation of the erogenous zones. We regard this as the onanistic theory of love.

References

Erikson, E. H. *Childhood and society.* New York: Norton, 1950.
Furchner, C. S., and Harlow, H. F. Preference for various surrogate surfaces among infant rhesus monkeys. *Psychonomic Science,* 1969, **17**, 279–280.
Rosenblum, L. A. The development of social behavior in the rhesus monkey. Unpublished doctoral dissertation, University of Wisconsin, 1961.
Sackett, G. P. Monkeys reared in visual isolation with pictures as visual input: Evidence for an innate releasing mechanism. *Science,* 1966, **154**, 1468–1472.

ATTACHMENT AND DEPENDENCE: SOME STRATEGIES AND TACTICS IN THE SELECTION AND USE OF INDICES FOR THOSE CONCEPTS

Jacob L. Gewirtz[1]

National Institute of Mental Health
Bethesda, Maryland

Introduction

The sometimes reciprocal reliance of one individual upon another — mother and child, teacher and pupil, lover and loved one — summarized over many responses, situations, and setting conditions, has often been labeled "dependence" or "attachment" ("bond," "affectional tie," "relationship"). Typically used ambiguously and often interchangeably, these abstract terms have labeled a broad area of scientific interest and summarized classes of functional relations in which one individual's behaviors are controlled by stimuli provided by the behaviors of another or others. The child's side of the patterned social behavior involved in the two-sided interaction process has comprised the arena in which many researchers have sought to identify how later social behavior can be affected by early experience, including experience in deficient or disrupted environments. Because of the pervasiveness of the S–R functions involved as well as the degree of disorganization (and concurrent change in response intensity) that can result from interference with them, this broad conception has become a central focus in diverse theories of social development. As such, it would represent an important frame for considering "communication and

[1] The writer expresses his appreciation to Laura Rosenthal and Danielle Spiegler for their dedicated assistance, and to Dr. Miriam K. Rosenthal for her comments about an early draft of this paper. The opinions expressed herein are those of the author, and do not necessarily represent the position of NIMH.

19

affect," the topic of this book. However, there is as yet little detailed information about the origins, nature, and course of human social development generally, much less about the phenomena classified under attachment and dependence specifically.

Some strategic and tactical considerations for the selection and use of indices of attachment and dependence are discussed in this chapter.[2] In view of the limited degree of specificity with which such concepts have ordinarily been used, and the consequent absence of close coordination between those gross terms and either empirical operations or theoretical assumptions, it is not surprising that they have not often been indexed or measured in any systematic, consensual manner. What appear to be fundamentally different phenomena are occasionally grouped under each concept, and yet the two concepts are often defined identically and employed interchangeably. Moreover, the sequential behaviors of the interaction chains, presumed to be characteristic of the concepts, have not yet been sufficiently detailed under the relevant theoretical approaches. Since analyses often emphasize only behaviors without specifying the stimuli that control them or the stimulus contexts in which they are observed (which would determine their theoretical meanings), many and diverse behaviors might appear to connote attachment or dependence, and to be reasonable indices of one or the other of the concepts, or simultaneously of both. In this frame, I have suggested that progress in understanding the processes at issue can proceed most efficiently when the concepts employed are operational and tied explicitly to observable events, rather than considered as anything more than abstractions that stand for classes of functional relations.

I have elsewhere proposed a functional approach to the concepts of attachment and dependence and a heuristic distinction between them, based on whether an individual's behaviors are under the control of stimuli from a particular person (attachment) or from a specific class of persons (dependence).[3]

---

[2] My treatment of this issue was begun in earlier papers (Gewirtz, 1969b, c). It is here further expanded to encompass a larger number of types of indices, the tactics of their use under various research strategies, as well as the conceptual artifacts to which certain tactics may lead. More complete treatments of the matters surveyed here will be available in two papers that are scheduled to appear subsequent to the publication of this chapter (Gewirtz, 1972a, b).

[3] Given the historical context in which the terms "attachment" and "dependence" have been applied and the classes of problems to which they are applied currently, I have argued for the heuristic value of an operational distinction between them. In a functional learning frame, I have suggested that these terms are presently best conceived as abstractions for sets of functional relationships involving the positive stimulus control over a wide variety of an individual's responses by stimuli provided either by a *class* of persons (dependence) or by a *particular* person (attachment) (Gewirtz, 1961, 1969a, b, c). That is, in dependence, an individual's behaviors are conceived to be controlled by a discriminative and reinforcing stimuli which may be dispensed by any member of a *class* of persons who share certain

Commensurate with a functional analysis, one theme stressed here is the necessity for determining the functional relations between stimuli (both antecedent and consequent) and behaviors. Thus, the general approach advocated here would be to determine which stimuli provided by the object-person(s) and which responses of the interacting individual are involved in the reciprocal-control learning process summarized by the attachment-dependence concepts. Although this chapter will focus on interactions between a child and an adult, similar to much of the research in the field, it is stressed that my discussion is not limited to any particular age range or to any particular interaction partners. For a great variety of purposes, therefore, it would be possible to study behavior systems that touch on a conception of attachment or dependence *without* invoking either concept. At the same time, stimulus-response phenomena like these could be relevant to several (even contradictory) theoretical conceptions of attachment or dependence. The discussion of considerations in the selection of indices of attachment and dependence can therefore proceed independently of any particular theoretical approach or distinction. For instance, the heuristic distinction I have proposed between the concepts attachment and dependence would qualify the discussion that is to follow only insofar

---

stimulus characteristics and among whom there is similarity of the stimuli provided (e.g., as those involved in gender, race, age, or caretaking routine). In contrast, in attachment, the efficacy of discriminative and reinforcing stimuli in controlling an individual's behaviors are conceived to depend upon the unique physical and/or behavioral characteristics of the *particular* "object" person dispensing those stimuli (e.g., his facial stimuli, tactile characteristics).

Stated briefly, the acquisition of the stimulus–response patterns connoting attachment or dependence is conceived to involve two simultaneous processes which can begin when an infant is helpless and relatively immobile: (1) the conditioning of the physical and behavioral characteristics of a particular person or class of persons as discriminative and/or reinforcing stimuli for the child; and (2) the reinforcement and maintenance of various of the child's behavior systems by the diverse stimuli provided by that person or class of persons. It is assumed that diverse distal and proximal events provided by a person or a class of persons, in addition to those directly related to organismic survival, could come to function as discriminative and reinforcing stimuli for numerous child behaviors and behavior sequences, such as involve approaching, tracking, smiling, and vocalizing. Furthermore, at various points in the sequence of the child's (physical and social) development, changes are assumed to occur in both the stimuli and responses involved in the interactions. It is also assumed that behaviors of the interacting object person or persons will come under the control of stimuli provided by the behavior and appearance of the child or class of children. Thus child and adult could be said to become mutually "attached" or "dependent," the label for the relationship under this heuristic conception depending only on whether the controlling stimuli are provided by an object-person who has acquired unique value or by a class of objects who share certain stimulus characteristics and from whom the provision of a stimulus is equally effective. These processes for the acquisition and maintenance of attachment and dependence are therefore assumed to be similar to, but independent of, one another. In this frame, dependence is *not* the generalization of attachment.

as any response indices employed would relate an individual's behavior to the stimuli from a single person or to those from any one of a class of persons.

The Historical Perspective

The concepts *attachment* and *dependence* have been approached in diverse ways through the years. Psychoanalysis and its derivatives have considered "attachment" in terms of cathexis, object formation, and object relations, the "object" being the instrumental person, typically the mother, through whom the "instinctual aim" is satisfied (Freud, 1905, 1914, 1926, 1931, 1938). Approaches to comparative animal behavior and ethology have emphasized observations of gregariousness, imprinting, and the ties developed between animals of some species and humans (Spalding, 1873; Lorenz, 1935; Harlow, 1958; Scott, 1960, 1967; Sluckin, 1965; Salzen, 1967). Recently, due to Bowlby's (1958, 1960a, b, 1968, 1969) impetus, psychoanalytic assumptions have been combined with ethological and, to a degree, cognitive conceptions (e.g., of Piaget, 1936, 1937; Miller, Galanter, & Pribram, 1960). In this frame, the "attachment" label has been used to stand for a child's "affectional tie," particularly with his mother. In a similar way, Harlow and his associates have used the terms "affectional attachment" (Harlow & Zimmermann, 1959) and "affectional system" that pass through a "comfort and attachment" stage (Harlow & Harlow, 1965, 1966) for behavior systems that, in the course of development, "bind" the macaque infant first to his mother and then to others. Similarly, Scott (e.g., 1967) has conceived of a "primary social relationship," "primary bond," or "social attachment" that develops in animals (including humans) independently of environmental stimulation, the only requirement being merely prolonged "contact" with the mother or others during the critical period for the species. As does Harlow, Scott appears to use the abstract concept of primary relationship or attachment to order the organism's behaviors with regard to others.

The term "dependence" (dependency) has been used only occasionally in psychoanalytic or ethological orientations, but has been considered primarily in the framework of conditioning theories. In learning-oriented approaches of the past quarter century, the term "dependence" (and occasionally also "attachment") has tended to encompass the diverse, presumably learned, traitlike social "motive" systems of post-Watsonian behaviorism (e.g., Shaffer, 1936) which had evolved to reflect the importance of experience, replacing the earlier "instincts" of McDougall's time (e.g., McDougall, 1908, 1923). Such treatment of the term "dependence" (and occasionally "attachment") has mainly emphasized some implications, for social-behavior outcomes of child rearing, of the conception of conditioned, secondary reinforcement which is central to laboratory research on instrumental conditioning (e.g., Whiting, 1944; Sears, 1951, 1963; Sears,

Whiting, Nowlis, & Sears, 1953; Gewirtz, 1954, 1956b, 1961, 1969c; Beller, 1955, 1959; Heathers, 1955; Sears, Maccoby, & Levin, 1957; Cairns, 1966). At times, conflict based on occasional nonreward (frustration), or even punishment, of dependent overtures has been conceived (as a drive or motive) to qualify that conditioned-reinforcement conception (Sears *et al.*, 1953). Recently, the assumptions of various learning approaches have been reconciled with the concepts and findings of comparative animal behavior studies (e.g., see Gewirtz, 1961; and especially Cairns, 1966, 1969).

Some Implications of the Varied Uses
of the Terms "Attachment" and "Dependence"

Because the conceptualizations of attachment and dependence have so often been varied, overlapping, and inexplicit, issues which could be relevant to both concepts have often been considered in relation to only one or the other term, but not both, in a seemingly arbitrary fashion. For instance, account has been taken of issues, concepts, and data stemming from the ethological tradition in connection with attachment (Bowlby, 1958, 1960a,b, 1968; Scott, 1967) but almost not at all in relation to dependence, for which conditioning concepts have been employed almost exclusively (e.g., Sears, 1951; Gewirtz, 1956b; Sears *et al.*, 1957; Sears, 1963). Furthermore, the term "dependence" has sometimes had the implication of an immature (or even psychopathological) relationship or one that is reliant on situational requirements, whereas the term "attachment" has been used with the implication of a more mature, enduring relationship (Ainsworth, 1969; Bowlby, 1969). Similarly, the tendency has been to employ "attachment" for research related to social behavior systems of both human and animal infants, whereas "dependence" has been applied almost exclusively in research on human social behaviors, particularly of nursery-school-age children. In addition, "attachment" has been used as a broad label for both the extent and the intensity of the overall pattern of a child's interaction with his mother, with equally broad abstract terms like "dependence" (social and instrumental) and "affiliation" serving as overlapping labels for behavior attributes that purportedly define attachment (e.g., Caldwell, Wright, Honig, & Tannenbaum, 1970). Similarly, a range of issues which could be relevant to both attachment and dependence have been taken up differentially under each concept. Those topics which have been considered more in connection with attachment than with dependence include comparative and developmental changes in response topography, critical periods (Scott, 1967), attachment as a precondition for or sometimes a result of identification [as was discussed in my analyses of imitation and identification (Gewirtz & Stingle, 1968; Gewirtz, 1969c)], and a mutuality of interaction effects (i.e., both the child and his parent—caretaker could become mutually "attached") in contrast to the usual child-oriented unidirectionality of dependence (in which typically only the child and not his interacting parent–caretaker would be scored for dependence). On the other hand, several matters may have been more characteristic of work on dependence: a greater amount of systematic research, investigation of the control over behaviors of social reinforcing stimuli, such as the spoken word "good" (Gewirtz & Baer, 1958a, b; Cairns & Lewis, 1962), and examination of interrelations among response indices (e.g., Sears *et al.*, 1953; Beller, 1955, 1959; Gewirtz, 1956a; Sears, 1963; Rosenthal, 1967a, b). Moreover, situational determinants have been noted that differentially control the behaviors considered relevant for dependence (e.g., external conditions of frustration, Whiting, 1944) and for attachment (e.g., when a mother prepares to depart or after a child's reunion with her, Bowlby, 1960a, b).

The survey and arguments that follow regarding indices of attachment or dependence are independent of the heuristic distinction between attachment and dependence that I have proposed (see Footnote 3, page 20), as well as of theoretical positions others have taken on this general topic. The points to be made are meant to be generic and, in principle, to apply to any theoretical approach.

Some Frequently Employed Indices of Attachment or Dependence

As abstract concepts that have been closely related neither to empirical constructs nor to theoretical postulates, attachment and dependence have been indexed, denoted, or measured by diverse groupings of arbitrarily chosen response classes. For the most part, these responses have been inflected by their situational (stimulus) contexts. In turn, each such response class could provide the basis for measures of different response attributes (e.g., latency, amplitude, probability). Also, overall summary statements may be devised for the combinations or patterns of behaviors grouped under each construct (for instance, to characterize the "strength" or "intensity" of attachment or dependence). In this chapter, I consider only in passing the issues of response measures, of the overall summary characterization of sets of responses, and of the developmental changes through which responses go. Instead, I emphasize, in their stimulus contexts, the identities (contents of) response classes that have been used to denote attachment, dependence, or both concepts. These behavior classes have included:

(a) Responses indicating *direct positive control* by the stimuli provided by an "object" organism, as used by Sears *et al.* (1953), by Sears, Rau, and Alpert (1965), by Ainsworth (1967, 1969), and by Rosenthal (1967a), and as I have emphasized (Gewirtz, 1954, 1956a, 1961). [These responses would include, for example, orienting and visual following, greeting, approaching, and responses that maintain nearness; touching, holding, hugging, clinging, scrambling over, and kissing; as well as other responses, including crying, that are maintained by attention or approval – the latter as used, e.g., by Cairns and Lewis (1962) and Gewirtz (1967, 1969d).]

(b) Responses indicating *differential recognition* of, or *preference* for, the stimuli provided by an object person relative to the stimuli another person provides, for instance differential smiling, vocalizing, or crying (Harlow & Zimmermann, 1959; Cairns, 1966, 1968; Ainsworth, 1967, 1969; Yarrow, 1967, 1969; Sackett, 1968, 1970).

(c) The *absence* of *exploratory and similar responses* in a novel context, in the presence of an object person, where those responses would be *incompatible with responses reflecting the positive control of stimuli from the object person.* [These responses would be incompatible in the sense of only one stimulus being in predominant control at any one time. Hence, instead of displaying exploratory responses (e.g., toward new toys), the child orients his behavior toward the object person (Ainsworth & Wittig, 1969). Another set of responses that may be included in this class is investigatory responses oriented to the object person (Bowlby, 1969).]

(d) Responses assumed to indicate *direct positive stimulus control, but only in particular stimulus-control contexts* [e.g., the use-of-mother-as-a-secure-base-for-exploration index of Harlow and Zimmermann (1959) and of Ainsworth (1967)] or when seemingly aversive events are being avoided [which might be termed "security-getting" responses and have been emphasized by Bowlby (1960b), Ainsworth (1967), and possibly also by Sears and his associates (1953) (insofar as the latter's "seeking reassurance" index of dependence is involved)].

(e) *Avoidance responses,* including facial sobering or interruption of an on-going act, at the approach or in the presence of strange persons or places, in a context where, even if an object person is present, no approach is made to him to avoid the stranger (e.g., Yarrow, 1967).

(f) *"Emotional" responses* (e.g., crying, whimpering, temper tantrums) or other behaviors that connote "distress" or "apathy" that may have been brought about by interference with a response sequence reflecting positive stimulus control. In the case of interference effected by separation from a mother figure, such responses are sometimes said to connote separation "anxiety" or to represent "protests" or "discriminative vocalizations." Insofar as these emotional responses are incompatible with the occurrence of responses reflecting positive stimulus control or of other responses (e.g., exploration), for the lack of a better label they may be termed "disorganization behaviors." Such indices have been used by Ainsworth (1964, 1967), Schaffer and Emerson (1964), Yarrow (1967), and Fleener and Cairns (1970).

The S–R criteria just listed have sometimes been grouped informally in terms of assumed developmental phases that reflect differential responsiveness to the object person (e.g., see Ainsworth, 1967; Yarrow, 1967). However, it has been noted that the S—R indices which happen to be chosen to define a "relationship" arbitrarily define the (developmental) point at which it can be said to be established (e.g., Yarrow, 1967). Furthermore, some of the responses involved, like smiles, laughter, and other indications of what are termed displays of "positive affect," have often been assumed to reflect such states as "happiness" or "joy" that have sometimes also been postulated to be relevant indices of an attachment or dependence (e.g., see Caldwell, Wright, Honig, & Tannenbaum, 1970; Sears, 1969). [I have discussed the role of such terms as "joy," and their translation into observable stimulus—response events in an analysis of the smile response (Gewirtz, 1965) and elsewhere (Gewirtz, 1968, 1971).]

The qualities of attachment and dependence, or the distinctions between them, have been discussed by some in terms of such behavior attributes as "intensity." Sears (1969) has recently distinguished between attachment and dependence on the basis that the former is, and the latter is not, characterized by "passion" (a term he has not yet operationalized). I have noted that a single conditioning paradigm can efficiently order the two behavior systems, without necessarily attributing such affective qualities to either system (Gewirtz, 1969a). It is therefore assumed here that since such qualities as intensity or passion could be used to characterize responses (of any content) under any one of the earlier-listed index classes, establishing separate categories for those characteristics would, for most purposes, be redundant with the index classes themselves. That is, it is assumed that the performance implications of the acquired stimulus-control features involved are already being reflected in the indices.

I have noted that there has been a lack of consensus as to which response classes are indices of attachment and which of dependence and, indeed, the heading under which a given response should be classified. Researchers on attachment (e.g., Bowlby, 1958, 1960a, b; Ainsworth, 1964, 1967) have emphasized criteria that fall under several of the headings mentioned earlier, while researchers on dependence (e.g., Sears *et al.*, 1953; Gewirtz, 1954, 1956b; Beller, 1955, 1959; Sears, 1963; Sears *et al.*, 1965) have emphasized indices falling mainly under the heading of responses indicating direct positive control (a) including control under limiting conditions (d) as in "seeking reassurance" (although such initiations may have a focused, attachment flavor, as when they are stratified by object as in Sears *et al.*, 1965). At the same time, an infant's crying or protest upon the departure of his mother or others, used as an index of attachment by Schaffer and Emerson (1964), and his crying upon the approach of "strangers" in different contexts, conceived as attachment behaviors by Ainsworth (1964, 1967) and by Yarrow (1967), among others, may fall under "avoidance" responses (e) or "emotional" responses (f), or even under responses indicating direct positive control (a) (as is seen later, insofar as such protests may have been extrinsically reinforced in those stimulus contexts).

Theorists have also employed indices from each of classes (a)—(f), but without indicating the basis for their choice of index combinations. Thus, Ainsworth (1967) employed 16 indices [several more than in earlier years (Ainsworth, 1963, 1964)], of which roughly half reflected positive stimulus control [approach (a)], three differential recognition [preference (b)], one exploratory behavior (c), two or three positive control, but in particular stimulus contexts, (d), one avoidance (e), and one emotional response upon mother's departure (f). In a not dissimilar vein, Bowlby (1969) has recently emphasized that the patterns of attachment might best be described in terms of several "forms of behaviour." These include behaviors that initiate interaction (e.g., greeting, approaching, touching, embracing, scrambling over mother figure, burying face in her lap, calling, talking, hands-up gesture, smiling); behaviors in response to interactional initiatives and that maintain interaction (e.g., the above-listed behaviors as well as watching); behaviors aimed at avoiding separation (e.g., following, crying, clinging); exploratory behaviors, especially when oriented to the attachment-object (e.g., mother); and withdrawal (fear) behaviors, especially when oriented to the mother-object (Bowlby, 1969, p. 334). These behaviors represent essentially the entire range covered by the six listed S–R classes [(a)–(f)].

The selection of combinations of response measures employed to characterize the "strength" or some other attribute of stimulus–response systems classified under attachment or dependence often appears to be arbitrary. Even so, for those purposes for which an overall summary statement is desired, there are several parameters that could be used, singly or in different combinations, to characterize the strength or intensity of an attachment or dependence pattern, irrespective of the particular number or type of indices employed. These could include

1. the range and/or number of behaviors under the stimulus control of a class of persons or of a particular person;
2. that number relative to the number of behaviors under the stimulus control of others;
3. the degree of positive stimulus control over each behavior system (for instance as indicated by response probability);
4. the number of stimulus settings in which the control process operates; and/or conceivably also
5. the degree of disorganization and/or the intensity of emotional behaviors that ensues from interference with the interaction (though, as I argue later, such disorganization measures will necessarily be indices of confounded, partly irrelevant, conditions).

Alternatively, if responses implying attachment or dependence are each under a different form of stimulus control function, an overall summary statement may obscure these differentiated patterns and thus be of limited utility.

Moreover, in many studies a number of variable classes implied by the attachment or dependence concepts and often employed by earlier researchers have been disregarded, without it being reported how the criteria that have been selected to replace them are considered to be either representative or uniquely appropriate. At the same time, the S–R indices (in whatever combinations) used in studies of attachment and of dependence could also be employed for *any* behavior system (although the choice and combinations of the indices would not be arbitrary for an explicitly defined system), and are therefore generic and not limited to, or unique for, either attachment or dependence. Indeed, even the (contents of the) behaviors involved, whether orienting, touching, talking or smiling, remaining near, or crying, being angry, fearful, or anxious, would *not* be unique to the attachment or dependence case. Thus, given the inexplicit way that dependence and attachment have been typically conceived in recent years, diverse responses could be used to provide plausible indices of each of them, and different indices or sets of indices from any or all response classes could be emphasized, depending upon the strategy and tactics of a particular theoretical approach.

Based on their tactical utility, I have argued for the greater use of direct over indirect indices of positive stimulus control over behaviors, for instance, positive responses to discriminative stimuli from "object" persons as opposed to disorganization responses (Gewirtz, 1961). For, while a high correlation would be expected between approach responses in the absence of aversive stimulation and approach responses in the context of avoiding some situation, the latter responses represent only a more complex instance of stimulus control of "attachment" or "dependence" behaviors. "Disorganization" (e.g., emotional, frustration) responses will necessarily be indices of confounded conditions, specifically the interrelated factors of

1. the strength of the response sequence blocked;
2. the value for the individual of the terminal reinforcer involved;
3. the degree to which a stimulus condition actually interferes with a response sequence;
4. individual thresholds for emotional responding and the particular emotional responses evoked by that interference.
5. the availability of potential alternative responses in the individual's repertory, and the relative strengths of those responses.

Given the nature of these factors, "disorganization" responses will constitute less direct and hence less efficient indices of the positive control acquired by the stimuli that an object person provides.

Furthermore, although it might be assumed that disorganization responses will occur as a function of the strength of the response sequence interfered with or blocked, the value of the reinforcer, and like factors (holding the magnitude of each interference condition constant), it is conceivable that such disorganization responses might be emitted only for higher "response-strength" values of the blocked sequence. Alternatively, while a proportionality might be assumed between the disorganization responses and the degree of interference (holding response-strength constant), it is possible that the disorganization response might not result from lower degrees of interference with the attachment or dependence behavior sequence (i.e., a threshold phenomenon might be involved). Moreover, emotional responses that often result from interference with approach-response sequences connoting attachment or dependence may themselves come under the control of the same discriminative and reinforcing stimuli that control those attachment or dependence behaviors. In such cases, these responses could function as *direct* indices of acquired stimulus control (e.g., operant crying). Knowledge of both the response content and the contextual-setting condition is therefore necessary for the appropriate classification of the behavior and the determination of its relevance under nearly all approaches. Thus, if the limitations of using approach responses that occur in the context of avoidance, and disorganization responses, are recognized by theorists, there are conditions under which they may constitute valid and useful attachment or dependence indices. There are also research contexts in which the efficient tactic would be to emphasize security behaviors or disorganization indices. This would be the case when the purpose of an approach is specifically to understand aversive stimulus control in natural settings, the disorganization brought on by interference with attachment or dependence behaviors, or disorganization generally, and not to deal directly with issues of positive stimulus control over relevant behaviors as such.

Before discussing in greater detail some tactical issues relevant to the determination of appropriate indices of attachment or dependence, some general points regarding the choice of indices and the methods of measurement should first be noted. It is an accepted principle that these two factors will determine the findings of any given study. A survey of the research done under the headings of attachment and of dependence reveals an unusual paucity of data replications among the studies, apparently due in part to differences in indices, in methods of measurement, and in samples studied (Maccoby & Masters, 1970). For example, Ainsworth (1963) and Schaffer and Emerson (1964) have both studied the age of onset of "specific attachments." However, Schaffer and Emerson concluded that "specific attachments" develop at a later age than that reported by Ainsworth. This discrepancy may be more than simply an outcome of the questionable tactic of using chronological age as the key independent variable in psychological research on developmental processes, as I have noted elsewhere (Gewirtz, 1969c, particularly pp. 105–119). (It is, after all, the details of the process occurring in time that are the concern of the psychologist.) What may be more pertinent here is the fact that different criterion indices were used by Ainsworth and by Schaffer and Emerson (Maccoby & Masters, 1970). Whereas Schaffer and Emerson measured attachment primarily in terms of separation reactions, Ainsworth employed a wider range of behavioral criteria. Other things equal, these two sets of indices may simply have shown different relationships to chronological age. (It is, of course, also possible that the difference was due to some other methodological difference between the two studies. For instance, the investigators may have merely sampled from different subject populations.)

It has also been noted by reviewers of attachment and dependence studies that different findings are obtained depending upon the method of measurement employed. For instance, with nursery-school-age subjects, five dependence measures, found to yield a pattern of reliable intercorrelations when teacher ratings were employed as the method of measurement (Beller, 1959), had almost no intercorrelations when similarly-labeled frequency-count measures were based on direct observation (Sears, 1963). More generally, as Maccoby and Masters (1970) have concluded after reviewing the literature, when rating scores are employed, dependency emerges as a "coherent dimension" having a fairly high degree of "trait consistency," but when observation-count scores are employed, a much more differentiated picture of dependency is obtained. Furthermore, while a prevalent method used in attachment or dependence studies has been to relate the earlier socialization practices of parents to the child's later behavior patterns connoting attachment or dependence, the number and dimensions of child-rearing practices studied and how they are measured in any given investigation will to a large extent determine the findings of a study. However, there are some major difficulties in the measurement of socialization practices that can determine research findings. For instance, a widely used method of evaluating parental practices or child responses is the retrospective interview or questionnaire report. However, such reports are of dubious validity and have come increasingly into question (e.g., see Hartup, 1963; Maccoby & Masters, 1970). Also, the variables these methods generate may be attenuated when measures are differentially reliable and overlap in meaning. Finally, the built-in interrelationships among the various socialization practices makes it extremely difficult to separate the effects of a given parental practice from other characteristics of parental behavior and the child's environment (e.g., see Sears *et al.*, 1953). Although, in principle, difficulties like these can be overcome, many researchers working in the area of dependence or attachment and employing such indices and methods of measurement have not yet come to recognize fully the role that arbitrarily chosen methods can play in determining result patterns.

Assumptions Often Underlying the Use
of Attachment and Dependence Indices

In research conducted under abstract conceptions like dependence and attachment, there are major strategic considerations involved in the choice of indices, as well as a number of tactical assumptions involved in the way those indices are used. Explicit recognition is almost never given to there being, under the routine conceptions of dependence or attachment, many and diverse potential indices of those concepts. But this factor should qualify inferences from any set of indices, however relevant they might be under a researcher's theory. An implicit and unwarranted assumption that is often made is that the various indices of either of the two concepts are alternative measures of a unitary attachment or dependence process, that, therefore, they should intercorrelate highly (in principle, perfectly), and that the coefficients comprising a single intercorrelation matrix should characterize all subjects in all situations. However, if, in a given situation or across settings, the responses generating the S–R indices are alternatives to each other or mutually exclusive, the indices need not intercorrelate in a simple way, or with the same sign, or even at all. Furthermore, by the very fact that such numbers of variegated measures are used for each concept, many of which may have been selected somewhat arbitrarily by earlier investigators [in the case of dependence, e.g., by Beller (1948) and Gewirtz (1948)], there is bound to be some overlap among these indices. Hence, any intercorrelations they yield could be due to this artifactual basis alone, if not also to rating biases or similar artifacts.

In principle, therefore, if theoretical terms are not well coordinated with empirical operations so that the sequences of environmental stimuli and child behaviors that are taken to characterize attachment or dependence are not described in sufficient detail, many and diverse behaviors might appear to be reasonable indices of attachment or dependence, singly or in various combinations. Yet, these variegated indices need not intercorrelate in a simple way, or even at all. Hence, an expectation of finding that one set of intercorrelation matrix values will characterize the index interrelationships for some group of randomly selected subjects may be an oversimplification. By the very nature of the life setting, it seems reasonable to suppose that the histories of individual children would differ in regard to each of the response systems comprising the subcategories that define such summary variables as dependence or attachment. Indeed, on this basis, a unique intercorrelation matrix for attachment indices, or dependence indices, might be expected for every group of subjects, insofar as each such group may have a different average stimulus–response chain pattern reflecting differences in the individual conditioning-history patterns involved.

For a group of children homogeneous in history, or within a particular setting, it is possible that there might be something like a standard stimulus–response interaction chain that characterizes their sequential attachment or dependence behaviors. However, as noted, large individual differences would be expected on the interrelationship of the variables among children not homogeneous in reinforcement history. That is, it is plausible that the behaviors of individual children would be organized according to quite different interaction-chain patterns, and that some responses typically used as indices may have a certain relation to other responses in the chain. For instance, one response may be a precondition or an alternative for another response. Thus, in the standard (and perhaps artificial) setting in which assessments are made, child A might be (misleadingly) scored higher on nearness behaviors and lower on behaviors connoting deviations for attention than child B, simply because the first response of child A to stimuli early in an attention-seeking chain pattern might be moving near while that of child B might be crying. Furthermore, at later phases in the learning process there may be a "short-circuiting" of the chain as it becomes more efficient, in that fewer behavior steps may come to be required for the child to attain attention, approval, or some other stimulus consequence. Moreover, if a response to a stimulus close to the end point of the chain is prevented from occurring, it is possible that the child would then employ with greater frequency a response which ordinarily would occur earlier in the organization of the sequence.

Another implicit and often unwarranted assumption is that the occurrence of a behavior index or measure is independent of the situations sampled. (This assumption appears to have underlain much early trait-concept usage, that averaged either child or environment responding across situations and setting conditions.) There is considerable evidence that situational contexts acquire differential discriminative control over child behaviors (Gewirtz, 1969b, 1972c). Therefore, as that assumption of independence between behavior and situations is seldom if ever tenable, behavioral data obtained, the intercorrelation matrices they form, and the conclusions drawn from them would be biased by the sample of behavior contexts that happens to be selected for study. It is plausible that the occurrence of a behavior would depend upon the imperatives and constraints in the situations represented and the relative response strengths based on the reinforcement histories of the subjects. A child who ordinarily exhibits consensually valued behaviors that are maintained by "positive attention" might exhibit negative deviations for attention when those around him are quite busy. Similarly, after exposure to a brief period of social isolation, children for whose behaviors social approval had acquired strong positive reinforcing value (as determined by a questionnaire) emitted relatively more "incorrect" responses that were (positively) reinforced by contingent disapproval connoting "negative attention" (hearing the visible experimenter say "you're wrong") than they emitted "correct" responses that were followed by a contingent flash of light (Gallimore, Tharp, & Kemp, 1969). Closely related to these points is the often neglected consideration that independently defined subcategories may overlap in (physical) stimulus qualities. Thus, it is difficult to conceive of a case when a child is held by an adult and is not simultaneously caressed or provided with behaviors that connote positive "attention," if not also with "approval" or "affection." It is the stimulus context in which a response is exhibited that will determine its meaning and theoretical relevance. Therefore, both response (content) and environmental situation (as well as contextual-setting conditions) must be specified and taken into account. What often seems to be missing from analyses using such indices, however, is an awareness of the importance of such factors and of factors like ecological constraints and imperatives or definitional overlap of behavior categories, a deficiency which can make researches on dependence or attachment artifactually complex as well as arbitrary and their findings most difficult to evaluate.

The particular situational conditions in which behaviors occur may also dramatically affect the operation of a chain. That is, in some environmental settings (such as those involved when a child is ill) one stimulus–response pattern could characteristically occur, while in another environmental setting (such as when a child is in a group that includes peers) a quite different organization of stimuli and responses could occur. Furthermore, the momentary setting conditions involved (such as when a child is hungry) would differentially determine the efficacy of stimuli and hence the behaviors for which they are discriminative or reinforcing. As some of the patterns enumerated could on occasion cancel others, or lead to the same end result, the matrix of index intercorrelations summarizing (averaging) these diverse relations could obscure the differentiated nature of the underlying patterns. Yet it is these patterns that are the primary focus of a functional analysis of the sequential relations between stimuli and responses. Hence, if only selected responses are observed in selected settings while the entire stimulus–response chain and its history are overlooked, an incomplete, even misleading, impression of the child's behavior pattern may be obtained.

The basic conditioning conception of a stimulus–response chain can illustrate some of the reasons why the subcategories of dependence or attachment would not be expected to relate to each other in a homogeneous way, or necessarily even at all, especially for groups of children selected for study without regard to their stimulus–response chain histories – to date, the characteristic mode of sampling. Therefore, subcategory intercorrelations, or those between gross summary indices like total dependence or attachment and, for instance, some "identification" score, may prove to be of little theoretical consequence when abstractions like dependence and identification are reduced to their component functional relationships involving acquired stimulus control over responses (Gewirtz & Stingle, 1968; Gewirtz, 1969c). Only at this level of a functional analysis can one avoid what are difficulties at the more abstract levels, for instance, the fact that individual children display different or opposite behavior patterns or that some emit behaviors which are accounted for by the indices used, while others do not. Consequently, generalizations about the relationship among the indices or between them and environmental settings would be limited due to these factors that would determine (bias) a particular intercorrelation matrix. Thus, knowledge of the different conditioning-history patterns of the individuals comprising a group of subjects, and an understanding of the stimulus and setting conditions operating in the situation, would be critical for the optimal comprehension and prediction of the pattern in which the dependence or attachment indices are organized.

Some Considerations Regarding the Number and Types of Indices to Employ

We have seen that many and variegated criteria of dependence and of attachment are in use. Although the use of several presumed indices of a process is not in itself detrimental, some limitations of using uncritically a large number of such indices have been noted. A convenient tactic often employed fruitfully in conditioning and other experimental analyses but seldom considered in the dependence–attachment research area has been to use a single S–R index and a single measure of that behavior. A single index can be convenient when it focuses the stimulus-control functions under investigation in one response and therefore precludes use of multivariate statistical procedures. Specifically, a single response class may be sufficient for a researcher's purposes if it is

1. reliable and generates a sufficient range of empirically consistent scores (a criterion for any measure);
2. representative of the stimulus control process under the researcher's conception;
3. functionally related to important independent variables under the researcher's theoretical expectations.

Hence, much has been made of studies which have explored the differential reinforcing efficacy of the spoken word "good" for discriminative child responding following short-term deprivation and satiation pretreatments (e.g., Gewirtz, 1967, 1969d, 1972c; Landau & Gewirtz, 1967). While laboratory studies of social discriminative and reinforcing stimuli connoting "attention" or "approval" and the responses they control have not ordinarily been considered related to attachment or dependence behaviors in life situations, such stimuli are often very similar to those maintaining behaviors classified under these two concepts. Hence, it should be instructive to examine the functional relationships into which these social stimuli enter [as Maccoby and Masters (1970) have done so well]. At the very least, they can illustrate the utility of using a single criterion index in research.

However, there are several reservations that should be noted regarding the use of small numbers of indices, particularly under an inexplicit or unfocused approach. It is possible that an attachment or dependence index based on a single response (or a small number of responses) in life settings may only reflect the conditioning history of a particular response system, and that system may be unrepresentative of the broader set of stimulus control functions characterizing the individual's repertoire. That is, the response could actually be under some special form of social stimulus control independent of (and irrelevant to) that implied by the attachment or dependence conception used. Furthermore, a single index might be extremely unrepresentative insofar as children might show rather little attachment or dependence by other criterion indices (that reflect either positive or negative stimulus control). Thus, the utility of a single index is limited by the difficulty of ensuring that it does not simply reflect idiosyncratic conditions in a child's unique conditioning history.

For instance, it has already been noted that Etzel and Gewirtz (1967) have shown that crying can be readily maintained (reinforced) by caretaker attention (i.e., hovering around the child, talking, picking him up), even in the early weeks of life. And various investigators have demonstrated how diverse other response based attachment indices used by some, and connoting attachment behaviors to others, can be instrumentally conditioned in the early weeks of life, which is also well before the time many would conceive that an "attachment" could have been acquired. These responses include eye contact, smiling, vocalizing, and crying (e.g., Brackbill, 1958; Rheingold, Gewirtz, & Ross, 1959; Weisberg, 1963; Etzel & Gewirtz, 1967). Also, the ages of onset and of the acquisition of selective stimulus control may vary with the differences in experience implied by diverse child-rearing settings (Ambrose, 1961; Gewirtz, 1965; H. B. Gewirtz & J. L. Gewirtz, 1969). Therefore, if a single "attachment" or "dependence" index is used, care must be given to rule out the possibility that the response reflects merely a history in which the child had been routinely reinforced for displaying that behavior generally, or in certain situations (for instance, whenever his mother was about to leave his vicinity), when that stimulus-control function is unrepresentative of those connoting attachment or dependence.

The way in which this type of artifact could impeach the implications of an investigation of attachment can be illustrated by a report of Schaffer and Emerson (1964). Those investigators employed several measures based on a single response index of attachment, measures that summarized the (con-founded) occurrence, intensity, and direction of infant protests (comprising whimpers, fusses, and cries) after seven different types of separations from their mothers and others.[4] Based upon mothers' reports, Schaffer and Emerson (1964) found that the "intensity of attachment-to-mother at 18 months [p. 50] " (measured in terms of the characteristic intensity of protests at separation) was a positive function of (a scale for) (a) the speed with which mothers respond

---

[4]It is interesting to note that Ainsworth (1963), who employed 13 behavior criteria in her study on attachment, found that the use of the single protest index was insufficient and (in terms of her findings) possibly even misleading. (Considerations in the use of a large number of indices were discussed earlier.)

to their infant's crying (initiations), and (b) the frequency, duration, and intensity of interaction initiated by the mother with her infant. Under a routine instrumental-learning conception, these results can suggest that the infants who protested (cried) most strongly at separation were those whose usual protest and crying behaviors were frequently, rapidly, and intensely (and, on these bases, most efficiently) reinforced by their mothers. Schaffer and Emerson (1964, p. 51) have themselves noted this possibility in discussing the relationship between attachment intensity and the speed of maternal responsiveness scale and, assuming they could not disentangle cause from effect in this context, chose to discount this explanation of their attachment measures.

Therefore, while they may otherwise index the child's strong "tie" to his mother, in cases like that of Schaffer and Emerson, the various measures of protests-in-separation situations may reflect only the limited fact that the mother had systematically reinforced crying-protest behaviors, particularly when she was about to leave her child. On such a basis, cues provided by the mother's (or others') preparations for departure from the infant would have become discriminative for his crying and fussing protest responses. Therefore, although such instrumentally-conditioned behaviors could serve as attachment measures that are assumed representative of the stimulus-control process in a functional analysis, they would seem to constitute artifacts or, at best, confounded rather than straightforward indices of attachment, that would have to be ruled out under a conception like that of Schaffer and Emerson. Indeed, differences in specific protest-training conditions, particularly in the discriminability of the unique cues provided by the object-mother when she prepares her departure, might account, at least in part, for the pronounced individual differences in the age of onset of "specific attachment" found by Schaffer and Emerson. A functional behavior-oriented analysis of the stimulus conditions that have acquired control over relevant responses of the individual could help to eliminate such confounding factors (whether single or multiple indices are used).

There is still another dimension to the issue of the choice of indices of attachment and of dependence. Although the tactics of different theoretical approaches to attachment and/or dependence will often differ, at the core of nearly all approaches is a concern with process, and therefore with the sequential details of caretaker—child interchanges (Gewirtz, 1969b). However, some researchers have occasionally used summarizing variables (e.g., overall dependence, strength of attachment) for the child's behavior, and sometimes also terms at similar levels of abstraction for indexing the assumed relevant controlling details of the environment.[5] This usage has sometimes been justified

---

[5] The role of such one-sided variables in research on the two-sided parent—child interaction process has been considered in detail elsewhere (e.g., J. L. Gewirtz & H. B. Gewirtz, 1965; Gewirtz, 1969b,c; H. B. Gewirtz & J. L. Gewirtz, 1969).

on practical grounds in preliminary investigations and by near-term tactical considerations (as a research short cut) in research on more differentiated issues.

In the frame outlined, the potentially more profitable approach being proposed here would be to determine which stimuli provided by the object-person(s) are or become effective in controlling the child's responses and which of his responses are maintained (reinforced) by those stimuli (and vice versa). A functional approach to the reciprocal-control conditioning process therefore attends to the details of the sequential patterning of the contingencies between environmental and behavioral events occurring in the interchanges between the child and his (caretaking) environment. This emphasis may not be dissimilar to Cairns' (1966, 1969), nor is it unlike Ainsworth's (1969) or Bowlby's (1969) emphasis upon the sequential details of interaction and upon the settings and conditions in which the observed behaviors occur. The importance of an emphasis like this is also recognized by Sears (1969), who agrees that such "global attitudinal qualities [as warmth and permissiveness do not] accurately reflect the really relevant variables, i.e., the contingencies of reinforcement and the precise behavior being reinforced [p. 14]." He therefore also stresses the relevance of an interaction analysis which details the specific stimulus conditions associated with a particular response as well as the reinforcement schedule related to each action.

As illustrated by some research in which I have been engaged (J. L. Gewirtz & H. B. Gewirtz, 1965; H. B. Gewirtz & J. L. Gewirtz, 1969), variables that summarize behaviors or stimulus events across contexts, or that are almost demographic in character (e.g., time a mother spends in interaction with or merely near her child in a given setting), can be reduced to patterns of environmental stimuli in contingent relations with child behaviors, in a developmental framework. A functional learning approach like this one thus emphasizes the sequential stimulus and response features of stimulus control, for both the acquisition and the maintenance of behavior, as well as the situational and setting–condition context of interaction (Gewirtz, 1967; 1972c). Under such an approach, there thus appears to be little need or reason to employ gross summarizing concepts like attachment and dependence, except to suggest the literature to which the findings are considered relevant. However, once the sequential details of the interchanges between stimuli and responses are identified, there are many ways in which they could be grouped by content or control function and summarized for different analytic purposes. These purposes might include: (a) detailing behavior patterns (including those connoting attachment or dependence) during the first year of life; (b) comparing widely different child-rearing groups; or (c) devising a strategy to foster socially desirable outcomes in interpersonal behavior. For each of these ends there could be some utility in attempting to identify types of social response patterns that occur at different points in a child's history, and in that sense, constitute developmental points or levels. Under some problem definitions for children in the first year of life, these patterns need not, in principle, differ markedly from the five phases that Ainsworth (1967) has concluded characterize the development of attachment of Ganda infants, nor need they differ from the five somewhat different social response patterns that Yarrow (1967) has concluded correspond to "levels of object relationship" in infants prior to and following their separation from foster mothers. Alternatively, the naturally occurring behaviors might be grouped according to a quite different principle under a different problem definition, such as the identification of ordered phases in a single response-based index. Hence, phases, levels, or patterns may be used to represent a more abstract order of response definition under any approach, even one oriented toward detailing the functional relations denoting stimulus control over response indices.

The basic point to be made is that there are purposes for which summary abstractions can have utility, insofar as they can organize efficiently the already identified sequential details of interactions. But when they do not do this, the use of such abstractions as "dependence" and "attachment" can obscure the fundamental characteristics of the processes loosely grouped under these rubrics. The emphasis of theorists using such gross abstractions has been primarily on summarizing behaviors. And even when the stimulus conditions that control and maintain such behaviors have been considered, it has often been only under gross abstractions, so that the moment-to-moment differences in behavior brought about by the moment-to-moment changes in the controlling stimuli have been obscured. Moreover, there have not often been attempts to tie closely presumed dependence or attachment behaviors as outcomes to various extreme conditions as antecedents. Research approaches in the past, even those employing a learning approach, have tended to rely on the method of studying generalized patterns of stimulation provided by the environment, such as those termed "nurturance," "consistency," and "frustration," and of relating them to general traits in the behavior of children, like those termed "dependency," "attention-seeking," and "insecurity" (Gewirtz, 1969b). Because such abstractions have tended not to focus on the sequential details of interaction, they have by their nature limited the analyses of both the stimulus conditions and the behaviors of the child: They have tended to index only some average characteristics of the behaviors and/or stimulus conditions through extended time spans, and have precluded the necessary articulation between the stimuli provided by the environment and the relevant behaviors of the child. That is, by dealing with the environmental stimuli and the child's behaviors under such generalizations, researchers have tended to neglect the sequential and contingent relationships of the discrete stimuli and the discrete responses. Therefore, such methods cannot help but miss the subtleties that some of the extant theoretical approaches would consider relevant and important.

The Empirical Literature and Attachment–Dependence Indices

The child development literature is replete with normative studies of age-related differences for a variety of behaviors oriented (differentially) to mothers and others, or evoked by "strangers" (e.g., Bühler, 1933, pp. 347–417; Shirley, 1933; Gesell & Thompson, 1934; Gesell, Halverson, Thompson, Ilg, Castner, Ames, & Amatruda, 1940). Studied at monthly or bimonthly intervals during the first year of life, these social behaviors include differential regard, recognition, or knowing of mothers, acceptance of "strangers" or sobering at, fearing, or withdrawing from them. The literature also contains reports of more focused investigations of many age-related social behaviors, for instance infant smiling to a human face (e.g., Washburn, 1929; Spitz & Wolf, 1946; Ambrose, 1961; Gewirtz, 1965), crying at monthly psychological examinations (Bayley, 1932), and crying at medical examinations (Levy, 1960). Moreover, almost all infant developmental or "intelligence" tests (e.g., Gesell, 1925, 1928; Bühler, 1930; Bayley, 1933, 1969; Cattell, 1940, 1960; Gesell & Amatruda, 1947, 1962; Gilliland, 1949, 1951; Griffiths, 1954) contain items that are similar to some of the social responses studied in normative researches. As these test items are derived from the response norms of standardization samples, their age placement could indicate at what monthly age-point children from the standardization groups of the tests characteristically exhibited the item response in the standard stimulus context used (holding constant the criterion of item placement used).

The age norms of a variety of such studies have been available for many years. However, investigators of the age course of often very similar responses, but as presumed indices of an "attachment" or "relationship" or of "dependence," have rarely even attempted either to compare their results to those of studies that did not use such labels, or to rationalize similarities or differences (e.g., see Ainsworth, 1963, 1964, 1967; Schaffer & Emerson, 1964; Yarrow, 1967). Furthermore, it has seemed that the age norms found in investigations carried out under the aegis of the attachment and dependence terms have been considered by many to be somehow more conceptually relevant or important than those of studies to which such labels have not been applied.

Investigations that have employed such rubrics as "attachment" and "dependence" have attempted in one way or other to emphasize a patterning of their criterion indices relevant to their concepts. Nevertheless, it is remarkable that the age functions for their heavily stressed criterion indices have typically been reported only in isolation, without being in any way related to what appear to be relevant earlier studies that have tabled age functions for very similar and sometimes seemingly identical indices (e.g., based on patterns of smiling, crying at separation, or withdrawing from strangers). Nor have those reports indicated how such operations as response definitions, methods of measurement, and samples differ (if indeed they do) from those of the earlier similar studies, how the age-related results differ (as they often do), and how these discrepancies may be explained (e.g., by sampling considerations). As a result, it has been difficult, if not impossible, for a reader to place the reported findings of each of these later studies of human attachment or dependence in a proper perspective, to permit evaluating their relevance not to mention their reliability.

Some examples can help us to appreciate the critical importance of this point. Yarrow (1967), Schaffer and Emerson (1964), and Ainsworth (1967) have each reported the age course of social behaviors that, at least at first glance, seem to be similar to some of those for which age norms have been reported by Gesell and Thompson (1934). Thus, Yarrow investigated "active recognition of mother" at 1, 3, and 5 months of age; and Gesell and Thompson studied "knows mother" at comparable age points. Similarly, Schaffer and Emerson reported the number of cases at successive age points who showed the onset of a "fear-of-strangers" (by crying, withdrawing, turning away, etc.); and Yarrow reported the percentage of subjects showing "stranger anxiety" (involving "active protest or withdrawal in the presence of a stranger [p. 436] "); while Gesell and Thompson employed the apparently similar index of "withdraws from strangers" (and of "sobers at strangers") as well as the reciprocal index of "accepts strangers." Yet neither Yarrow nor Schaffer and Emerson anywhere related their studies or findings to those of Gesell and Thompson (or others) nor, what may be equally important, indicated their reasons for not thus "anchoring" their studies in the literature.

A comparison that I have made of some age-related results of the respective investigations, however, reveals both similarities and differences. For instance, Yarrow's index of "active recognition of mother" yielded similar results to the Gesell and Thompson index of "knows mother," whereas Yarrow's index of "stranger anxiety" showed poor agreement with the Gesell and Thompson index of "withdraws from strangers" but reasonable agreement with their index of "accepts strangers." Had such similarities and differences been at least noted by Schaffer and Emerson or by Yarrow, and had an attempt been made to explain them (where necessary), it would be easier for readers to put their reported findings into the proper perspective: The reliability of the age-related results of their criterion indices could be better appreciated, and a sounder foundation would be provided for appreciating the conceptual implications of the social response patterns emphasized by those authors [for instance, in Yarrow's case, the (five) types of social response patterns that he has posited correspond to different levels of focused object relationship].

Moreover, even though several of the researchers cited often relate the response patterns studied to developmental levels or the age course of behaviors, there has seldom appeared to be an adequate empirical basis for their statements.

Where the percentage or number of subjects showing a given response (e.g., sobering at the appearance of a stranger) or passing a given test item are charted by chronological age in normative studies, it is rare for the attempt to be made to relate an individual's performance on an item at one age point to his performance on that same item at an earlier age point, or to his performance on some other item at the same or at an earlier age point. Thus, even in those studies that are longitudinal, there is no attempt to relate the sequencing of the appearance of responses in the same individual.

Finally, although many researchers of age-related social behaviors have often referred their indices to a conception of "attachment" (or "focused relationship") or of "dependence," such labels do not necessarily make their studies or findings more conceptually relevant than those that involve the same indices, but do not employ such labels. Thus, both Yarrow (1967) and Gesell and Thompson (1934) employed similar indices, but Yarrow related his findings to a conception of "focused object relationship" (attachment) while Gesell and Thompson conceived they were studying merely "social behaviors." In this connection, a colleague and I have reported the age course and environmental-group differences for such seemingly key social behaviors as differential smiling (as well as of vocalizing, watching, and crying), in sequential interchange with several key behaviors of the caretaking environment. In the process of studying those consensually meaningful child behavior systems, we found no compelling conceptual reason or tactical necessity for grouping these behavior results under, or referring them to, a superordinate concept like attachment or dependence. Though this tactic was open to us, we thought it might obscure some differential features of the response patterns we detected (Gerwirtz, 1965; J. L. Gerwirtz & H. B. Gewirtz, 1965; H. B. Gewirtz & J. L. Gewirtz, 1969). In contrast, it is recalled that Ainsworth (1967) employed differential smiling as an attachment behavior.

Thus, the decision to refer a set of functional relations to a superordinate concept like "attachment" or "dependence" has often been one of strategy (more than of tactics). Nevertheless, an all-too-frequent consequence of such an entirely legitimate conceptual decision has been the deemphasis of the functional S–R relations detected. As a result, such findings have been contributing far less than they should have been to the literatures of the behavior systems involved. This is regrettable in a conceptual context where those approaches that have been thought to give detailed and specialized developmental accounts of attachment or dependence are only now beginning to detail the conceptual bases for the selection of some types of the indices they employ, though not yet for all their number. We must keep in mind that the addition of a conceptual label to the results of a study neither changes them, accounts for differences between studies, nor necessarily makes one study more relevant than another. At the level of S–R criterion indices, empirical findings remain just that, regardless of the concept label to which they are referred.

Recapitulation

In this contribution, I have taken note of the various ways in which the abstract terms "attachment" and "dependence," closely related neither to empirical constructs nor to theoretical postulates, have been used. I then surveyed the great variety of cued response classes that have been employed to index attachment or dependence. These often seemingly arbitrarily chosen indices have included combinations of approach behaviors (including those reflecting differential preference or recognition, and approach behaviors in the context of avoidance) as well as emotional-disorganization behaviors [including those following interference with (approach) behavior sequences]. In the frame of this variegated usage, I detailed some considerations for the selection of indices under different research strategies and tactics, regardless of the particular theoretical orientation involved.

The importance of employing variables that attend to the sequential stimulus and response details of environment—child interaction was emphasized, and it was argued that positive responses to discriminative stimuli from object persons or classes of persons would most directly reflect the control process connoted by the terms "attachment" or "dependence." Even so, purposes were noted for which responses reflecting approach in the context of avoidance, (emotional) disorganization responses following interference with approach behavior sequences, or even single responses thought to be representative under a given theoretical approach, might constitute meaningful and potentially useful attachment or dependence indices. It was emphasized that the criterion indices employed by theorists to characterize the "strength" or some other attribute of dependence or attachment could be used for almost any behavior system. For a great variety of purposes, therefore, it would be possible to study behavior systems that touch on a conception of attachment or dependence *without* invoking either concept. Indeed, it was thought that progress in the direction of accumulating functional relations to characterize the processes at issue could proceed most efficiently in terms of operational concepts closely linked to observational data. However, it was also noted that the individual's responses can be grouped in terms of such criteria as content or control function, depending upon a researcher's theoretical purpose. On this basis, it is also possible to identify phases, levels, or patterns that represent a more abstract order of response definition, even under an approach oriented toward detailing the functional relations denoting stimulus control over responses.

Several assumptions that often underlie the use of indices, and that qualify their validity, were noted and critically examined. An implicit but unwarranted assumption that is frequently made is that the various (often arbitrarily chosen) indices of attachment or of dependence are alternative measures of the same unitary process and that, therefore, the coefficients of a single homogeneous intercorrelation matrix should characterize all subjects in all situations. Furthermore, it is also often unjustifiably assumed that the occurrence of a behavior (index) is independent of the settings sampled. However, the conception of a common stimulus–response chain can illustrate some reasons why the subcategories of dependence or of attachment should not be expected to relate to each other in a homogeneous way, or necessarily even at all. Therefore, knowledge of the different conditioning-history patterns of the individuals comprising a group of subjects, and an understanding of the stimulus conditions comprising the situation sampled, were thought critical for the comprehension and prediction of the intercorrelation pattern in which the dependence or attachment responses are organized.

Several tactical and strategic considerations regarding the number of indices to employ were also discussed. While it was noted that the uncritical use of a large number of indices could have detrimental consequences, it was also pointed out that the use of several presumed indices of a process is not in itself detrimental, if the possible consequences of this practice and the complexities involved are taken into consideration. Moreover, given the inexplicitness of most present approaches to attachment and dependence, the potentially useful practice of employing a single criterion index and a single behavior measure was considered to have several limitations. For example, the cued response might be extremely unrepresentative of the individual's social repertory and could actually be under some special form of social stimulus control independent of (and irrelevant to) that implied by a researcher's conception of attachment or dependence. It was proposed that a functional behavior-oriented analysis of the stimulus conditions that have acquired control over relevant responses of the individual could help to eliminate confounding factors that qualify the inferences that may be drawn from any (set of) indices.

Related to the issue of the choice of indices of attachment and of dependence is the frequent use by researchers of summarizing variables for the child's behaviors and also for indexing through time the assumed relevant details of the environment. While this tactic is occasionally warranted under strategies focused on process (which effectively includes almost every contemporary approach), the alternative approach outlined in this paper urged increasing attention to the sequential and contingency details of stimuli and responses in the interaction between the child and his environment, for both the acquisition and the maintenance of (classes of) behavior. Under such an approach, there are a large number of practical ways in which the identified sequential details of the interchanges could be organized. For most conceptual purposes, however, a functional approach would minimize the need for gross summarizing concepts like attachment and dependence. Such an emphasis would therefore avoid some difficulties encountered when attachment or dependence are conceived as inexplicit, gross abstractions and are (more or less) arbitrarily indexed by criteria that may involve confounding factors, that may not be representative, or that may preclude a focus on the interrelationships between the stimuli provided by the environment and the relevant behaviors of the individual.

References

Ainsworth, M. D. The development of infant–mother interaction among the Ganda. In B. M. Foss (Ed.), *Determinants of infant behaviour II.* London: Methuen (New York: Wiley), 1963. Pp. 67–112.

Ainsworth, M. D. Patterns of attachment behavior shown by the infant in interaction with his mother. *Merrill-Palmer Quarterly*, 1964, 10, 51–58.

Ainsworth, M. D. S. *Infancy in Uganda: Infant care and the growth of love.* Baltimore: Johns Hopkins Press, 1967.

Ainsworth, M. D. S. Attachment and dependency: A comparison. Paper presented at the biennial meeting of the Society for Research in Child Development, Santa Monica, California, March 1969.

Ainsworth, M. D. S., & Wittig, B. A. Attachment and exploratory behavior of one-year-olds in a strange situation. In B. M. Foss (Ed.), *Determinants of infant behaviour IV.* London: Methuen, 1969. Pp. 111–136.

Ambrose, J. A. The development of the smiling response in early infancy. In B. M. Foss (Ed.), *Determinants of infant behaviour.* London: Methuen (New York: Wiley), 1961. Pp. 179–201.

Bayley, N. A study of the crying of infants during mental and physical tests. *Journal of Genetic Psychology*, 1932, 40, 306–329.

Bayley, N. *The California first-year mental scale.* Berkeley, California: Univ. of California Press, Syllabus Series No. 243, 1933.

Bayley, N. *Bayley scales of infant development: Birth to two years.* New York: Psychological Corp., 1969.

Beller, E. K. Dependency and independence in young children. Unpublished Ph.D. thesis, State Univ. of Iowa, 1948.

Beller, E. K. Dependency and independence in young children. *Journal of Genetic Psychology*, 1955, 87, 25–35.

Beller, E. K. Exploratory studies of dependency. *Transactions of the New York Academy of Sciences*, 1959, 21, 414–426.

Bowlby, J. The nature of the child's tie to his mother. *International Journal of Psychoanalysis*, 1958, 39, 1–34.

Bowlby, J. Ethology and the development of object relations. *International Journal of Psychoanalysis*, 1960, 41, 313–317. (a)

Bowlby, J. Separation anxiety. *International Journal of Psychoanalysis*, 1960, 41, 89–113. (b)

Bowlby, J. Effects on behaviour of disruption of an affectional bond. In J. M. Thoday & A. S. Parkes (Eds.), *Genetic and environmental influences on behavior*. Edinburgh: Oliver & Boyd, 1968. Pp. 94–108.

Bowlby, J. *Attachment*. London: Hogarth (New York: Basic Books), 1969.

Brackbill, Y. Extinction of the smiling response in infants as a function of reinforcement schedule. *Child Development*, 1958, 29, 115–124.

Bühler, C. *The first year of life*. New York: John Day, 1930.

Bühler, C. The social behaviour of children. In C. A. Murchison (Ed.), *Handbook of child psychology*. (2nd ed. revised) Worcester, Massachusetts: Clark Univ. Press, 1933. Pp. 347–417.

Cairns, R. B. Attachment behavior of mammals. *Psychological Review*, 1966, 73, 409–426.

Cairns, R. B. Modification of social preferences in children and young animals. Paper presented at the meeting of the American Psychological Association, San Francisco, September, 1968.

Cairns, R. B. Attachment and dependency: Toward a psychobiological alternative. Paper presented at the biennial meeting of the Society for Research in Child Development, Santa Monica, California, March 1969.

Cairns, R. B., & Lewis, M. Dependency and the reinforcement value of a verbal stimulus. *Journal of Consulting Psychology*, 1962, 26(1), 1–8.

Caldwell, B. M., Wright, C. M., Honig, A. S., & Tannenbaum, J. Infant day care and attachment. *American Journal of Orthopsychiatry*, 1970, 40, 397–412.

Cattell, P. *The measurement of intelligence of infants and young children*. New York: Science Press, 1940; Psychological Corp., 1960.

Etzel, B. C., & Gewirtz, J. L. Experimental modification of caretaker-maintained high-rate operant crying in a 6- and a 20-week-old infant (*Infans tyrannotearus*): Extinction of crying with reinforcement of eye contact and smiling. *Journal of Experimental Child Psychology*, 1967, 5, 303–317.

Fleener, D. E., & Cairns, R. B. Attachment behaviors in human infants: Discriminative vocalization on maternal separation. *Developmental Psychology*, 1970, 2, 215–223.

Freud, S. Three contributions to the theory of sex. In A. A. Brill (Trans.), *The basic writings of Sigmund Freud*. New York: Modern Library, 1938. Pp. 553–629. (Originally published in 1905.)

Freud, S. On narcissism: An introduction. *The standard edition of the complete psychological works of Sigmund Freud*. Vol. XIV. London: Hogarth, 1957. Pp. 73–102. (Originally published in 1914.)

Freud, S. Inhibitions, symptoms and anxiety. *Standard edition*. Vol. XX. London: Hogarth, 1959. Pp. 87–172. (Originally published in 1926.)

Freud, S. Female sexuality. *Standard edition*. Vol. XXI. London: Hogarth, 1961. Pp. 225–243. (Originally published in 1931.)

Freud, S. *An outline of psychoanalysis*. London: Hogarth, 1938.

Gallimore, R., Tharp, R. G., & Kemp, B. Positive reinforcing function of "negative attention." *Journal of Experimental Child Psychology*, 1969, 8, 140–146.

Gesell, A. *The mental growth of the preschool child*. New York: Macmillan, 1925.

Gesell, A. *Infancy and human growth*. New York: Macmillan, 1928.

Gesell, A., & Amatruda, C. S. *Developmental diagnosis: Normal and abnormal child development, clinical methods and practical applications*. (2nd ed.) New York: Hoeber, 1947; (3rd ed.) New York: Harper, 1962.

Gesell, A., Halverson, H. M., Thompson, H., Ilg, F. L., Castner, B. M., Ames, L. B., & Amatruda, C. S. *The first five years of life: A guide to the study of the preschool child*. New York: Harper, 1940.

Gesell, A., & Thompson, H. *Infant behavior: Its genesis and growth.* New York: McGraw-Hill, 1934.

Gewirtz, H. B., & Gewirtz, J. L. Caretaking settings, background events, and behavior differences in four Israeli child-rearing environments: Some preliminary trends. In B. M. Foss (Ed.), *Determinants of infant behaviour IV.* London: Methuen, 1969. Pp. 229–252.

Gewirtz, J. L. Succorance in young children. Unpublished Ph.D. thesis, State Univ. of Iowa, 1948.

Gewirtz, J. L. Three determinants of attention-seeking in young children. *Monographs of the Society for Research in Child Development*, 1954, **19** (2, Serial No. 59).

Gewirtz, J. L. A factor analysis of some attention-seeking behaviors of young children. *Child Development*, 1956, **27**, 17–37. (a)

Gewirtz, J. L. A program of research on the dimensions and antecedents of emotional dependence. *Child Development*, 1956, **27**, 205–221. (b)

Gewirtz, J. L. A learning analysis of the effects of normal stimulation, privation and deprivation on the acquisition of social motivation and attachment. In B. M. Foss (Ed.), *Determinants of infant behaviour.* London: Methuen (New York: Wiley), 1961. Pp. 213–299.

Gewirtz, J. L. The course of infant smiling in four child-rearing environments in Israel. In B. M. Foss (Ed.), *Determinants of infant behaviour III.* London: Methuen (New York: Wiley), 1965. Pp. 205–260.

Gewirtz, J. L. Deprivation and satiation of social stimuli as determinants of their reinforcing efficacy. In J. P. Hill (Ed.), *Minnesota symposia on child psychology.* Vol. 1. Minneapolis, Minnesota: Univ. of Minnesota Press, 1967. Pp. 3–56.

Gewirtz, J. L. The role of stimulation in models for child development. In L. L. Dittmann (Ed.), *Early child care: The new perspectives.* New York: Atherton, 1968. Pp. 139–168.

Gewirtz, J. L. A distinction between dependence and attachment in terms of stimulus control. Paper presented at the biennial meeting of the Society for Research in Child Development, Santa Monica, California, March, 1969. (a)

Gewirtz, J. L. Levels of conceptual analysis in environment–infant interaction research. *Merrill-Palmer Quarterly*, 1969, **15**, 7–47. (b)

Gewirtz, J. L. Mechanisms of social learning: Some roles of stimulation and behavior in early human development. In D. A. Goslin (Ed.), *Handbook of socialization theory and research.* Chicago: Rand-McNally, 1969. Pp. 57–212. (c)

Gewirtz, J. L. Potency of a social reinforcer as a function of satiation and recovery. *Developmental Psychology*, 1969, **1**, 2–13. (d)

Gewirtz, J. L. Stimulation, learning, and motivation principles for day-care settings. In E. H. Grotberg (Ed.), *Day care: Resources for decision.* Washington, D.C.: U.S. Office of Economic Opportunity (Pamphlet 6106-1), 1971. Pp. 173–226.

Gewirtz, J. L. Attachment, dependence, and a distinction in terms of stimulus control. In J. L. Gewirtz (Ed.), *Attachment and dependency.* Washington, D. C.: Winston, 1972. (Distributed by J. Wiley, New York.) Pp. 139-177. (a)

Gewirtz, J. L. On the selection and use of attachment and dependence indices. In J. L. Gewirtz (Ed.), *Attachment and dependency.* Washington, D. C.: Winston, 1972. (Distributed by Wiley, New York.) Pp. 179–215. (b)

Gewirtz, J. L. Some contextual determinants of stimulus potency. In R. D. Parke (Ed.), *Recent trends in social learning theory.* New York: Academic Press, 1972. Pp. 7–33. (c)

Gewirtz, J. L., & Baer, D. M. Deprivation and satiation of social reinforcers as drive conditions. *Journal of Abnormal & Social Psychology*, 1958, **57**, 165-172. (a)

Gewirtz, J. L., & Baer, D. M. The effect of brief social deprivation on behaviors for a social reinforcer. *Journal of Abnormal & Social Psychology,* 1958, 56, 49–56. (b)

Gewirtz, J. L., & Gewirtz, H. B. Stimulus conditions, infant behaviors, and social learning in four Israeli child-rearing environments: A preliminary report illustrating differences in environment and behavior between the "Only" and the "Youngest" child. In B. M. Foss (Ed.), *Determinants of infant behaviour III.* London: Methuen (New York: Wiley), 1965. Pp. 161–184.

Gewirtz, J. L., & Stingle, K. C. Learning of generalized imitation as the basis for identification. *Psychological Review,* 1968, 75, 374–397.

Gilliland, A. R. *The Northwestern Intelligence Tests. Examiner's manual. Test A: Test for infants 4–12 weeks old.* Boston: Houghton Mifflin, 1949.

Gilliland, A. R. *The Northwestern Intelligence Tests. Examiner's manual. Test B: Test for infants 13–36 weeks old.* Boston: Houghton Mifflin, 1951.

Griffiths, R. *The abilities of babies: A study in mental measurement.* New York: McGraw-Hill, 1954.

Harlow, H. F. The nature of love. *American Psychologist,* 1958, 13, 673–686.

Harlow, H. F., & Harlow, M. K. The affectional systems. In A. M. Schrier, H. F. Harlow, & F. Stollnitz (Eds.), *Behavior of nonhuman primates.* Vol. 2. New York: Academic Press, 1965. Pp. 287–334.

Harlow, H. F., & Harlow, M. Learning to love. *American Scientist,* 1966, 54, 244–272.

Harlow, H. F., & Zimmermann, R. R. Affectional responses in the infant monkey. *Science,* 1959, 130, 421–432.

Hartup, W. W. Dependence and independence. In H. W. Stevenson (Ed.), *Child psychology: The sixty-second yearbook of the National Society for Study of Education, Part I.* Chicago: Univ. of Chicago Press, 1963. Pp. 333–363.

Heathers, G. Acquiring dependence and independence: A theoretical orientation. *Journal of Genetic Psychology,* 1955, 87, 277–291.

Landau, R., & Gewirtz, J. L. Differential satiation for a social reinforcing stimulus as a determinant of its efficacy in conditioning. *Journal of Experimental Child Psychology,* 1967, 5, 391-405.

Levy, D. M. The infant's memory of inoculations: A contribution to public health procedures. *Journal of Genetic Psychology,* 1960, 96, 3–46.

Lorenz, K. Companionship in bird life. In C. H. Schiller (Ed.), *Instinctive behavior.* New York: International Univs. Press, 1957. (Originally published in 1935.)

Maccoby, E. E., & Masters, J. C. Attachment and dependency. In P. H. Mussen (Ed.), *Carmichael's manual of child psychology.* (3rd ed.) Vol. 2. New York: Wiley, 1970. Pp. 73–158.

McDougall, W. *An introduction to social psychology.* (30th ed.) London: Methuen, 1950. (Originally published in 1908.)

McDougall, W. *Outline of psychology.* New York: Scribner, 1923.

Miller, G. A., Galanter, E., & Pribram, K. H. *Plans and the structure of behavior.* New York: Holt, 1960.

Piaget, J. *The origins of intelligence in children.* New York: International Univs. Press, 1952. (Originally published in 1936.)

Piaget, J. *The construction of reality in the child.* New York: Basic Books, 1954. (Originally published in 1937.)

Rheingold, H. L., Gewirtz, J. L., & Ross, H. W. Social conditioning of vocalizations in the infant. *Journal of Comparative & Physiological Psychology,* 1959, 52, 68–73.

Rosenthal, M. K. Effects of a novel situation and of anxiety on two groups of dependency behaviours. *British Journal of Psychology,* 1967, 58, 357–364. (a)

Rosenthal, M. K. The generalization of dependency behaviour from mother to stranger. *Journal of Child Psychology & Psychiatry*, 1967, 8, 117–133. (b)

Sackett, G. P. Innate mechanisms, differential rearing experiences, and the development of social attachments by rhesus monkeys. Paper presented at the meeting of the American Psychological Association, San Francisco, September, 1968.

Sackett, G. P. Unlearned responses, differential rearing experiences, and the development of social attachments by rhesus monkeys. In L. A. Rosenblum (Ed.), *Primate behavior: Developments in field and laboratory research.* Vol. 1. New York: Academic Press, 1970. Pp. 111–140.

Salzen, E. A. Imprinting in birds and primates. *Behaviour*, 1967, 28 (3–4), 232–254.

Schaffer, H. R., & Emerson, P. E. The development of social attachments in infancy. *Monographs of the Society for Research in Child Development*, 1964, 29 (3, Serial No. 94).

Scott, J. P. Comparative social psychology. In R. H. Waters, D. A. Rethlingshafer, & W. E. Caldwell (Eds.), *Principles of comparative psychology.* New York: McGraw-Hill, 1960. Pp. 250–288.

Scott, J. P. The process of primary socialization in canine and human infants. In J. Hellmuth (Ed.), *Exceptional infant: The normal infant*, Vol. 1. Seattle, Washington: Special Child Publications, 1967. Pp. 469–514.

Sears, R. R. A theoretical framework for personality and social behavior. *American Psychologist*, 1951, 6, 476–483.

Sears, R. R. Dependency motivation. *Nebraska symposium on motivation: 1963.* Lincoln, Nebraska: Univ. of Nebraska Press, 1963. Pp. 25–65.

Sears, R. R. Attachment, dependency and frustration. Paper presented at the biennial meeting of the Society for Research in Child Development, Santa Monica, California, March, 1969.

Sears, R. R., Maccoby, E. E., & Levin, H. *Patterns of child rearing.* Evanston, Illinois: Row, Peterson, 1957.

Sears, R. R., Rau, L., & Alpert, R. *Identification and child rearing.* Stanford, California: Stanford Univ. Press, 1965.

Sears, R. R., Whiting, J. W. M., Nowlis, V., & Sears, P. S., in collaboration with E. K. Beller, J. C. Cohen, E. H. Chasdi, H. Faigin, J. L. Gewirtz, M. S. Lawrence, & J. P. McKee. Some child-rearing antecedents of aggression and dependency in young children. *Genetic Psychology Monographs*, 1953, 47, 135–234.

Shaffer, L. F. *The psychology of adjustment.* Boston: Houghton Mifflin, 1936.

Shirley, M. M. *The first two years: A study of twenty-five babies. Intellectual development.* Vol. 2. *Personality manifestations.* Vol. 3. Minneapolis, Minnesota: Univ. of Minnesota Press, 1933.

Sluckin, W. *Imprinting and early learning.* Chicago: Aldine, 1965.

Spalding, D. A. Instinct, with original observations on young animals. *Macmillan's Magazine,* 1873, 27, 282–293. (Reprinted: *British Journal of Animal Behaviour*, 1954, 2, 2–11.

Spitz, R. A., & Wolf, K. M. The smiling response: A contribution to the ontogenesis of social relations. *Genetic Psychology Monographs*, 1946, 34, 57–125.

Washburn, R. W. A study of the smiling and laughing of infants in the first year of life. *Genetic Psychology Monographs*, 1929, 6, 397–535.

Weisberg, P. Social and non-social conditioning of infant vocalizations. *Child Development,* 1963, 34, 377–388.

Whiting, J. W. M. The frustration complex in Kwoma society. *Man,* 1944, **115**, 140–144.
Yarrow, L. J. The development of focused relationships during infancy. In J. Hellmuth (Ed.), *Exceptional infant: The normal infant.* Vol. 1. Seattle, Washington: Special Child Publications. 1967. Pp. 429–442.

TWO PROBLEMS IN COGNITION:
SYMBOLIZATION, AND FROM ICON TO PHONEME

David Premack

Department of Psychology
University of California
Santa Barbara, California

Symbolization: More Primitive Than Language

Symbolization – the representation of one item by another item – either for the sake of one's self (for internal processing) or for the sake of communicating with another organism – is too basic a process to have begun with language. More likely, language modified existing structures rather than introducing a wholly new form of cognition. Thus, language may have (1) increased the ability to process temporal order; (2) added a second channel to memory or perhaps only enhanced one that was already there; (3) extended short-term memory by allowing rehearsal; (4) generally enhanced the ability to operate upon mental events. But these are all quantitative modifications.

The main cognitive equipment needed for present-day thinking existed prior to the evolution of language; it was present in prelanguage man, and is evident in the contemporary ape. The more colorful version of this hypothesis is that the qualitative difference between man and ape is phonological, not semantic or even syntactic. In a sense, I shall defend this thesis here – not at all because I can prove it, and certainly not because I believe it, but because the opposite assumption has become a cliche, and it is time to see whether that cliche can be supported by evidence, or whether its main virtue is familiarity.

Let us begin by examining the individual components into which cognition can be analyzed, and then weighing the comparative evidence for each. The components include (1) mental images; (2) analysis of an object into its features; (3) concepts of both the physical and functional variety, for example, color as a physical concept, animate—inanimate as a functional one; (4) displacement: the

51

ability to generate an internal representation of an object in the absence of the object and to utilize that internal representation; (5) subjective organization in memory; (6) clustering in memory; (7) rule induction, i.e., the attempt to induce a rule or structure that will generate a set of exemplars; (8) presumptive linguistic operations, such as deletion, rearrangement, many to one substitution.

Regrettably, for most of these cases there is presently no comparative evidence to weigh. But because that is so I will avoid the customary assumption which seems to be that if the component has been demonstrated in man, but not elsewhere, it is therefore found only in man. There is also the opposite side of this tendency, which is even more insidious. Limitations are discovered in chimps, such as Köhler's (1927) conclusion that in fashioning a tool the chimp is more likely to tear a metal pole from a wall than break a branch from a tree because the pole is isolated visually from its surroundings while the branch is not. Rather than test children on the same kind of problem, to see whether their inventions, too, might be constrained by similar perceptual factors, the assumption is made that the limitation is unique to infrahumans. The need for a test is apparently dismissed on the grounds that one has only to glance at the tools man has invented in order to appreciate that his inventions could not be constrained by similar factors. But there are at least two things wrong with this comparison. First, it compares the immature chimp with the human adult. Second, and more important, man is represented, not by the output of an individual in an experimental session, but by the cumulative glory of human culture. The impression given is that the computer, gas engine, steam shovel, and finest surgical tools are representative of what every human being is capable of, whereas the best the chimp can do is put a few sticks together. Few practices contribute more to the sense of qualitative rather than quantitative difference than that of contrasting the performance of an individual chimp with the whole of human culture. The comparison is additionally foolhardy, because we know that in both human and infrahuman populations, inventions are the accomplishment of a few individuals, and that in the human case, every generation has the advantage of all preceding inventions.

Moreover, the fact of culture cannot itself be taken as evidence of a qualitative difference, since culture is not the result of capacity alone but of capacity operated upon by environmental constraints. The effect of such constraints can be seen even in the present-day chimpanzee. In the Gombi Stream Reserve, chimps make simple tools and eat meat and insects [Goodall, 1965; actually, tool making and insect eating in the chimp was reported as early as 1927 (Köhler)]; whereas in the deep rain forests they have not been observed to engage in these behaviors (Reynolds & Reynolds, 1965) (however, the reported wariness of chimps shown by the Colobus monkey, one of the species chimps eat in the Gombi Stream Reserve, suggests that the frequency of meat eating in the rain forest is more likely low rather than zero; too low to have been observed by man but not so low as to have escaped the notice of the victim species). Before attributing these behavioral differences to genetic factors, we should take into account the greater abundance of fruit in the deep rain forests. In sum, to avoid the unjustified impression of a qualitative difference, comparisons cannot reasonably contrast the culture of a whole genus with the output of an individual. One individual must be compared with another individual and at comparative ontogenetic stages.

Although we are now collecting data on most of the cognitive components already enumerated, so far we can speak about no more than a very few of them. Those that will concern us here have to do mainly with symbolization. I have already defined this process as the representation of one item by another item. There is some impression that symbolization entered with the development of language. But this impression can be corrected by showing that symbolization is within the capacity of the chimp and, indeed, in all likelihood, the dog. We are in a better position to prove the former than the latter, although data that may prove the latter do not appear to be far off.

An African-born female chimpanzee (named Sarah), when about 6 years old, was taught various language-like performances (Premack, 1971). An analog of a written language was used both to circumvent the short-term-memory problem and to permit a training procedure in which the basic operation was one-to-one substitution. Words, the elemental unit in the system, consisted of pieces of plastic that differed from one another on a multidimensional basis. They were backed with metal, and adhered to a magnetized slate. Sentences were written on the vertical.

Words and linguistic forms taught her include class concepts, such as color, shape, and size; the copula; the quantifiers, all, none, one, and several; the logical connective if–then; negation; the metalinguistic use of language, and the compound sentence. But we are not interested in the chimp's overall linguistic competence, only specifically in its ability to symbolize, to represent reality to itself. What evidence can we find along these lines? Can a chimp generate an internal representation of an object in the absence of an external representation? We have two sources of evidence, one informal, discovered inadvertently at an early point in training; the other more formal, a product of deliberate tests made later in training.

At an extremely early point in training, Sarah was taught the names of fruits. Tests of her knowledge of the fruit names were made by offering her one piece of fruit in the presence of two fruit names. Her performance was disappointing. Given a piece of, say, apple, in the presence of the words "apple," and "raisin," she was only somewhat above chance in her correct use of the word "apple." And this was the case for many of the other fruits. In time, it dawned on us that these "errors" might not be errors (a failure to associate a name with a fruit) but requests for a preferred piece of fruit that was not present on a given trial. We tested for this possibility by establishing a preference ordering for the fruits and for the corresponding words. Sarah was given paired comparisons on a set of five fruits and independent paired comparisons on the corresponding set of words. The concordance between the two preference orderings was of the order of .8, ruling out that her apparent errors were based on a failure to have developed the intended association between the fruit and the plastic word. Her use of a word to request a fruit that was not present suggests that she was capable of generating a representation of the fruit in the absence of it. More conclusive tests of this point were made later in training.

"Color of" "name of" and "shape of" were used productively, i.e., to generate new instances of themselves. Thus, once she had been taught "name of" it was possible to use this concept to teach her new names. In similar fashion it was possible to introduce new color names with the concept "color of." "Color of" had been taught her originally as the relation between red and apple, and between yellow and banana, all four words having been established in previous training. In effect she was asked, "What is the relationship between red and apple?" and given the answer "color of," i.e., "red color of apple." The same answer given her in the case of yellow and banana led her to produce "yellow color of banana" — the second of the two positive exemplars that were used characteristically in teaching her all concepts. The two negative exemplars which were also standard were formed by re-pairing the positive cases, e.g., "red not color of banana" and "yellow not color of apple." Her comprehension of the concept was shown by her ability to apply "color of" to exemplars that were not used in training. Thus she could say that the relation between, say, red and cherry, was also one of "color of" (rather than "shape of," "size of," or "name of") (Premack, 1971).

But she could go beyond merely applying a concept to exemplars not used in training; she could use the concept to generate new exemplars. In the case of "color of" this was seen in the introduction of the new color names, "brown" and "green." For instance, she was given the instruction, "brown color of chocolate." "Brown" was the only new word, both "color of" and "chocolate" having been established earlier. (In the same lesson, she was also given "green color of grape" as the second positive case, and "brown not color of grape" and "green not color of chocolate" as the two negative cases.) She was then presented with four wooden disks, only one of which was painted brown, and told "take brown." She was consistently correct in her choice of the brown disk. Since the instruction "brown color of chocolate" was given her at a time when chocolate was not present, and she was subsequently able to select the brown object, she must have been able to generate an image of chocolate in the absence of the object on the basis of the word alone. The ability to talk about objects not present, or to utilize information about such objects, is an example of what Hockett (1959) called "displacement"; he cited it as an important design feature of human language in contrast to animal call systems. Displacement is a hallmark of language, but is apparently not unique to man. Moreover, the present example shows not merely that Sarah is apparently capable of mental images but, of additional importance, that she is capable of using them.

The information can be made still more precise, however, by including controls – the need for which escaped our attention on the first round of tests. Of the disks offered Sarah, only one was brown. However, brown was also the only characteristic property of chocolate (as Sarah knew it) that was instanced by the disk. A more informative test requires that the alternatives offered contain a number of the characteristic properties of chocolate, such as those of size, shape, texture. Then, if Sarah still chooses the brown disk, she could be said to be choosing exactly the color of chocolate and not just any property associated with chocolate. We plan to redo the test, because if done with the more rigorous controls, it can tell us not only that the chimp is capable of forming and using mental images, but of using them in highly specific ways. Fortunately, even the weak test shows that the chimp is capable of generating images and of using them.

How does an animal represent an object to itself? How it does so in fact is a question more difficult than we can answer, but how it could do so in principle is more nearly within reach. We start by asking whether or not an animal is capable of analyzing a complex object, such as an apple, into features. If the answer is yes, then one way in which it could represent such an object to itself would be as a conjunction of features.

We used match-to-sample to find out whether or not the chimp could do a features analysis on an apple. Sarah was given a series of trials in which she was presented with an apple and a pair of alternatives. On each trial she was required to indicate which alternative was more like the apple. The alternatives used were red versus green, round versus square, square with stem-like protruberance versus plain square, and round (no protruberance) versus square with protruberance. The alternatives in this first analysis were objects instancing the properties; in later analyses words were substituted for objects as her vocabulary permitted, e.g., she was required to decide whether the apple was more like "red" or "green" rather than the red or green patch used in the first test. Sarah was indeed capable of consistently analyzing apple (and other objects) into features, and features that coincided with the human analysis.

After obtaining a features analysis of the apple, we repeated the test exactly, except for replacing the apple with the word for apple. Once again, Sarah was required to indicate whether the object that the word represented was, for example, red or green, round or square. Although the word for apple was not a red apple itself, but a piece of blue plastic, she assigned to the plastic the same features she earlier assigned to the apple (see Fig. 1).

Thus, her analysis of the word was not of its physical form, but of that which

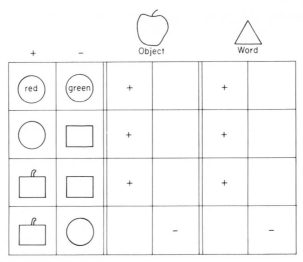

Fig. 1. Features analysis of the object apple, and the word "apple." (From D. Premack, Language in Chimpanzee?. *Science,* May 21, 1971, **172,** 808–822, Fig. 7. Copyright 1971 by the American Association for the Advancement of Science.)

the form represented. In short, in the presence of the word, Sarah was able to generate the features of the referent of the word. We do not know the necessary and sufficient conditions for this effect, or even the exact point in training when the effect first becomes demonstrable. Consider two major alternatives:

1. In the course of acquiring language, the organism learns to symbolize.
2. Symbolization is an integral property of perhaps all learning and makes language possible.

The second assumption seems more reasonable, since it does not require the further assumption that it is possible to teach an organism that does not symbolize in the first place to symbolize. It may be possible, but I do not see how, any more than I can see how to teach an organism that does not transfer to do so.

What form would symbolization take in lower organisms if the second assumption were true? An informal, nonlaboratory example, may be more clarifying at this point than a formal example. A dog nosed a leash in the hallway. Is a walk into the house or out of it? Into the fields or into town? With birds or without? Squirrel scent or not? Etc. When asked these questions of the walk, in one case, and of the leash, in the other, the dog's answer should be the same.

Recently we have begun to make such tests with dogs and birds, in general, to extend procedures designed for the chimpanzee to lower species. Unfortunately, we are not far enough along to say whether or not the bird or dog can symbolize. But in the case of the dog, our preliminary information would seem to increase the prospects of this possibility to a degree that was not anticipated.

As formulated here, evidence for symbolization consists of three main performances. First, the subject must be able to do generalized match-to-sample, i.e., to make sameness–difference judgments over an unrestricted set of objects. Second, the subject must be able to analyze objects into features. Third, to a stimulus that is associated with an object – that serves to predict the occurrence of the object – the subject must be able to associate the same features that it associates with the object itself. Suppose a dog is taught that it can obtain a favorite ball by bringing the trainer a striped block (but that to obtain a bowl of water, it must bring a dotted block). To say that the dog is using the block as a symbol for ball requires showing that the features into which the dog is capable of analyzing the ball can be given by the dog not only in the presence of the ball, but also in the presence of the block alone. If the animal associates the same features to both the ball and the block of wood we would say not only that the wood is associated with the ball – that is a procedural fact – but also that the block stands for the ball.

Of the three procedures described, two dogs – of the three so far tested – have learned the first two. Both dogs have proven capable of making generalized sameness–difference judgments, and both have been shown capable of analyzing an object into its features. The specific objects used so far were a tennis ball and a frisbee. The dogs were capable of analyzing the ball in terms of the following alternatives: round versus square, soft versus hard, ball size versus larger-than-ball size, ball size versus smaller-than-ball size, coarse texture versus smooth texture, ball smell versus no ball smell. Dogs have not yet been taught to operate upon an arbitrary object in order to get the ball – to bring the trainer a striped block rather than, say, a plain one. But we know from other evidence that such a task involves an elementary form of learning and should give the dog no problem. (Indeed, Sir John Lubbock, a 19th century British naturalist, reported an experiment of this kind in *Nature* in 1884. Needless to say, we will want to replicate Lubbock's results, though I can say that his experiment appears to have been quite properly designed, to have included appropriate controls, and in that sense to be entirely legitimate.) In sum, the dog is apparently capable of generalized match-to-sample; capable of analyzing an object into its features; and almost certainly capable of operating upon an arbitrary object in order to obtain another object. All that remains to be shown is that the features which the dog assigns to a target object, it can also assign to the object which it uses to get the target object. If that outcome once seemed remote, it no longer does. In view of the already demonstrated capacities of the dog, symbolization no longer seems a distant step.

Two very different kinds of conclusions can be drawn from these speculations. According to the first, we have greatly oversold the uniqueness of man. True, we differ qualitatively from other organisms in the matter of language, but we differ only quantitatively in the general manner in which we process information. Symbolization, for example, is a more primitive mechanism than we have supposed. Though elaborated into richer forms by language, it is not dependent upon language. Its existence in at least rudimentary form can be shown in chimpanzee, even perhaps in dogs, in any case, in species that do not have language. That obviously is the conclusion I have pressed here. But a second conclusion is also possible. According to it, we are indeed unique, but we do not know how. We have stressed the wrong things. We have yet to discover the precise form of our uniqueness. This is the more gratifying conclusion, the one I consider more likely, and the one I intend to continue trying to prove. However, success is not guaranteed, and each time a supposed uniqueness fails to materialize, another conclusion is possible.

From Icon to Phoneme

The iconicity of language has come in for renewed study. The evidence includes a number of sound—meaning correlations, some apparently restricted to a relatively few languages but others possibly universal (e.g., Durbin, 1971); parallels between sentence word-order and the order of events described by the sentence (Westcott, 1971); parallels between perceptual figure—ground relations and the location of stress in the sentence. Is this evidence for iconicity surprising?

In face of the human (and infrahuman) disposition to imitate, one can only answer no. Even though there is no fully acceptable theory of the origin of imitation, the strength and pervasiveness of the disposition is unquestioned. Some of the most convincing evidence comes from observational learning. There is apparently no motivational process that cannot be produced on a purely observational basis. Reward, punishment, avoidance, extinction, etc. are typically carried out by operating directly upon the subject. But they can also be carried out indirectly by arranging that one individual observe another whose behavior is being modified by the direct procedure (e.g., Bandura, 1969). Thus a given response can be increased in one individual by rewarding actual occurrences of the response; but the same response can be increased in a second individual merely by arranging that he observe the first individual. One can reasonably argue that most of social behavior is learned in this indirect way.

But the case in which one individual duplicates the behavior of a second individual is a special case, and imitation need not involve two individuals. Imitation can occur in a single individual, either when he observes and duplicates the essential features of his own behavior, or more interestingly, when he duplicates one form of experience with another form. The simplest form of the latter is the mental image; Piaget and Inhelder (1971) argue persuasively that the mental image is not a mere by-product of perception but is a form of imitation. In forming an image one can be said to be repeating the essential features of an earlier experience in a somewhat different form. The change in form, and even the transformation that the image may impose upon the perceptual experience, does not in any way differentiate it from what is involved in observational learning. In both cases, there is an internal representation of an earlier experience, a partial duplication of that experience. It seems just as reasonable to treat the image itself as imitation as it does to treat the overt behavior that sometimes follows and is guided by the internal representation. Thus, the iconicity of language merely corroborates a disposition that is attested to on a variety of fronts.

Far more surprising than the icon is the phoneme. Unlike the iconic aspects of language, which merely carry out the imitative disposition, the phoneme occurs in opposition to that disposition. Indeed, the phoneme and its written counterpart, the grapheme, are not only noniconic, but totally nonrepresentational. How did language, which is pervaded with iconicity, develop a level that is noniconic? How did it go beyond this to a level that is nonrepresentational? The problem, in brief, is to explain the origin of the phoneme in the face of the opposing tendency to represent experience iconically.

Let me say at the outset I cannot solve this problem. At best, I can offer a few suggestions as to how certain characteristics of human language may have contributed to the solution of the problem.

In looking at the phoneme or premorphemic level of language, I make two assumptions. First, such a level was necessary to solve the "large world" problem. It would be grossly inefficient if not impossible for man to attempt to store a number of undifferentiated responses sufficient to map or name a "large" world. Even 500 such responses is a stern challenge, let alone the 5000 or 50,000 which more nearly represents the average lexicon of various age groups today. This problem can only be solved by a combinatorial approach, i.e., by generating 50 or so undifferentiated responses, systematic combinations of which make up the word or morphemic level of the language.

Second, I assume — without being able to prove — that there is no feasible way of reconstructing the world from meaningful pieces. That is, the combinatorial approach seems able to solve the "large world" problem only if units that go into the formation of words are not themselves representational. It is amusing to toy with the opposite possibility. Take a system of iconic gestures — visual or auditory — break them into subunits, arrange that each subunit retain a representational quality, and then try to build the diverse objects and events of the world from a combination of such units. By no means am I able to prove that it cannot be done. But all my attempts to date have resulted in systems that are almost immediately unwieldy.

To get a nonrepresentational level to the language, we need to find psychological processes that run counter to imitation and which, if strong enough, can produce outcomes opposite to it. There are at least two processes that could have this effect. Both are reasonably well founded and both, interestingly, can be shown nicely in a simple experiment contrasting the behavior of autistic and nonautistic children.

In a sense the autistic child carries the imitative disposition to its extreme. In his speech, provided he is not mute, he repeats whatever is said to him. Sometimes the repetition is of something said to him only a moment earlier, and sometimes of things said to him hours or even days earlier. But even in the delayed material the imitative character of the utterance is clear. What the child says in these cases bears little if any relevance to the situation that obtains. "Don't go now, Mary. I don't want to see you in here now, Mary. You wash your hands, Mary," is an actual quotation from a classically autistic child as she stood in the laboratory prior to the start of a familiar training session. With a knowledge of the child's life it would probably not be hard to reconstruct the circumstance that gave rise to each of the utterances – to picture the actual adult speaking as well as the pressures that stood behind the adult. It is also possible to invent factors that would lend some relevance to the child's utterances. Thus, a training session and some of the routines in the living quarters have common elements, supervisorial adults if nothing else. Washing hands in both situations may not be unreasonable. But the question of appropriateness is not important. Even if the child's utterances are thought to have a high degree of appropriateness, there is no basis for denying that they are imitations of previously heard speech, since there is little evidence for generated as opposed to imitative speech in the autistic child. He may have two kinds of utterances – one in which the external situation plays a relatively large discriminative role, another in which it plays a small role. But the utterances do not differ in imitativeness, and can probably be traced back to adult models in both cases.

The echolalic character of autistic children's speech seems to pose a paradox. He is deficient not only in speech but in social behavior generally; his lack of conversation is thus only one aspect of a larger deficiency. But if he is so imitative in speech or verbal behavior why is he not equally imitative in nonverbal behavior? Social behavior is said to be learned primarily on the basis of imitation, i.e., by copying adult or peer models. How then is a child imitative in speech so utterly devoid of social behavior? Is it because the imitativeness is confined to speech and does not carry through into the child's nonverbal behavior? That seems unlikely, but in any case it is worthy of test.

Some years ago R. Metz and I, who were then studying the language of institutionalized children at Camarillo State Hospital, devised a test of the possible disparity between the autistic child's imitativeness in verbal behavior and nonimitativeness in nonverbal behavior. On the basis of a simple speech test, we divided a group of eight institutionalized children into subgroups that were high and low for echolalia. Children in the high group reproduced the experimenter's statements about 85% of the time; the corresponding figure for children in the low group was only about 5%. So although all the children were institutionalized, only half of them were markedly imitative in speech. The two groups were matched for age and ranged in age from 6 to 12.

Recall that the point of this excursis is to show at least two psychological processes that can compete with imitation. To see these processes consider an object such as a horse, in fact a wooden miniature replica of a horse (since this is easier to deal with in the laboratory than a real horse). The processes to be illustrated bear no relation to horse as such, and could be shown by any other object. A wooden horse was simply one of our actual stimuli.

Consider the first of several ways in which the play horse can be operated upon. Suppose we cut the toy in half so there is a front end and a back end. The child is given either half of the horse essentially as the sample in a match-to-sample problem. The alternatives available to him include both the front end and back end of the horse. In the nonecholalic child we see the first of the two processes that are counter to imitation. The child who does not imitate speech does not imitate in the perceptual domain either. If the head of the horse is set before him he *completes* the animal by adding the back portion; he does the same if the back portion is set before him. In both cases, he completes the horse. The echolalic child, on the other hand, does not complete, but repeats the portion that is placed before him. (He can be induced not to do this by a combination of training and manipulation of the alternatives; when the object that made imitation possible was removed from the set, we found that the echolalic child was capable of completion, but that this response was suppressed by the stronger tendency to imitate.) In brief, children who are imitative in speech are also imitative in nonverbal behavior — so there is no paradox of the kind suggested. But keep in mind the main point of the example — the process of completion. Generally the process runs counter to imitation. Doubtless there are some cases where the two tendencies cooperate; where the addition of an already present element will extend a pattern to some more or less predetermined number and in that way serve to complete the figure. But generally, completion and duplication would seem to be opposing tendencies. And in any case, in the laboratory we can put them into opposition.

Completion can take weaker forms than that involved in the restoration of the horse. This is simply to say completion, too, has degrees. Presumably weaker examples of completion used in our test with the children involved such things as jars and their lids and forks with missing tines. The disposition to complete is perhaps weaker in these cases, because a jar without a lid (and a fork without a tine) is closer to being complete than is half a horse. This suggests also that we could have modulated the disposition to complete by cutting the horse at different points.

A still weaker case of completion is that given by two objects each of which is complete but which typically are found in association with each other. A horse and a saddle are an example. Likewise, cup and saucer; they were also used in the test, specifically, to compare the proportion of trials on which two halves of a cup were put together with the proportion on which a cup and a saucer were joined. (The former was greater than the latter, though not reliably so in our small sample.)

When two objects, each complete in itself, are put together, we can call this *association* rather than completion. But to do so may suggest a distinction where none really exists. In putting together a cup and a saucer, or a salt and a pepper shaker, or a horse and a saddle, we can still talk of completion though now the completion is of a figure rather than of a single object. We revive an old controversy: Which is the primary process, association or completion? Can we not discount completion by showing that in all such cases, the parts that subjects put together are those they have experienced together on many previous occasions? This argument seems strained when we come to such things as severed horses and disconnected silverware. What is the subject's actual experience with the dismembered version of these objects? Suppose, moreover, that subjects will reconnect fragments of objects that they never experienced as fragments. If so, an association argument would require holding that the recognition of an object involves a hypothetical decomposition of the object into its potential parts (which are infinite in number). Is that to be considered a part of normal perception?

On the other hand, the attempt to swallow association with completion encounters equal difficulty, especially if the attempt is made to assert natural (e.g., geometrical) lines along which completion is most likely to occur. It would seem that *any* two objects can be made to assume the quality of a figure merely by being experienced together. But this fact is less upsetting to a completion argument if the geometrical aspect of the argument is surrendered. An enthusiastic completion proponent can hold that this is so because the mind is extremely adept at inventing relational schemata. *Any* items experienced together can be made the arguments of *some* predicate, and the mind will not rest until it finds a suitable predicate. Moreover, the mind has a very large inventory of predicates.

The burden of the argument for the present problem is that both completion and association run counter to imitation. Association is more general than completion. The items that can be bound together through contiguity need not be incomplete. In principle, any pair of items can be associated.

I assume that language went through three phases. In the first, one item was represented by another item. In a second, the representation was by manual gestures. And only in the third was the representation vocal (Hewes, in press). (This assumption like the others to follow is entirely speculative: the underlying intuition is that the cognitive distance between one object and another is less than that between a gesture and an object, and thus that representation involved a weaker transformation in the one case then in the other.) But these phases were overlapping rather than separate. So we can picture strings or sentences in which objects and gestures occur together: gestures and sounds, and quite likely, objects, gestures, and sounds.

It also seems reasonable to suppose that message length increased greatly over the three phases, and that it did so primarily because situations were mapped in increasing detail. A hunting expedition, for example, may have been represented initially as such, and by a single object. Later, however, the event was decomposed into animals hunted, location of hunt, agents hunting, and was then represented not by one sign but by several. The pressure for this increase in mapping could come from two sources. Most simply, from an increase in the actual number of items that could serve as class members; for instance, an increase in number of species hunted, tools used in hunting, and strategies of hunting. Second, from an increasing competence in the ability to symbolize.

Of course, a further reason for supposing that symbolic communication went on for a substantial period before taking its present vocal form is contained in the first section of this chapter. The capacity for symbolization is apparently present in species that do not have language. Although capacity does not entail use, witness the chimpanzee, we need only assume appropriate environmental constraints to convert capacity into performance. Thus in the case of primitive man, I assume that pressures for symbolic communication preceded the evolution of speech sounds.

The practical advantages of a vocal medium are fairly obvious, they have been dealt with in numerous places, and I will not repeat them here. Rather I will look at possible psychological consequences of shifting from the two earlier forms of representation to a vocal form. Consider, first, the pressures that would be introduced by an increase in message length, and how these pressures would be met by a vocal medium. Both gestural and vocal representation would tax short-term memory, in contrast to representation by objects. And the problem would be aggravated by an increase in message length. But while the problem would apply equally to the gestural and vocal forms, the latter would appear to have unique resources for solving the problem.

First, the vocal medium seems to allow for a unique degree of rehearsal and thus for the perpetuation of previously heard messages. Although one could also engage in covert gestures, thereby protracting their duration, this could preclude the use of the limbs for other purposes and thus be nonadaptive. Second, a vocal medium would serve memory by allowing the parallel storage of visual images and their auditory representations. To appreciate the advantage of this arrangement consider Sarah, who is trained in a visual language. In her case, parallel storage would require that words no less than their referents be stored as visual images – a task seemingly more likely to exhaust channel capacity than the intermodal one.

In addition to serving memory, I assume that the vocal medium may make a critical contribution to the noniconic properties of language and thus ultimately to the evolution of the phoneme. Not the vocal medium per se, but the disparity between this medium and the visual one in which man primarily perceives his world. If the language modality and that of the primary perception of the world did not differ, the language may very likely have ended up iconic. The only arrangement that could fully guard against the iconic possibility would be a disparity in modality, a difference in the channels in which the language is expressed and the world is perceived. Thus a primarily visual organism like man would require an auditory or at least a nonvisual language; an auditory organism, if there were one, might end up with a visual language.

Both representation by objects and by manual gestures would retain the possibility of a language in which signs tended to recreate referents. A disparity in modalities would eliminate strict iconicity, taking us one step closer to the phoneme. But how do we take the next step? In the first step, we passed from iconic to largely noniconic but still representational units. We must now move from noniconic, but representational, units to units that are not even representational.

One suggestion as to how this might have come about is contained in the development of writing systems, where, fortunately, we have the advantage of a developmental record (Gelb, 1963). Original writing systems were thoroughly iconic, pictures or at least sketches of the items named. The pictographs, in at least some languages, tended to become increasingly less representational, until the symbols were conventions, and their meanings could not be told by visual inspection. Another development, called phonetization, occurred in tandem with the abstraction of the visual forms. In this process, objects that were difficult to represent visually came to be represented on a phonetic basis by a homonym. Suppose the season "spring" were to be represented by a visual symbol. This is more difficult than visually representing spring as a coil of metal. Accordingly, in phonetization "spring," the season, would be represented by the word for a coil of metal. At this point, we have objects that are represented on a purely visual basis (whether iconic or noniconic), but others whose representation is mediated by sound. Nevertheless, phonetization is still representational. That is, the phonetic symbol is still meaningful; in the case of our example, it means both season and coil of metal. However, phonetic symbols were the last step before the truly meaningless set of units – the syllabary and still later the alphabet. How was this last step taken?

Unfortunately, the last step is not one I can make explicit. But deal with it as an invention or discovery, since it is not unlikely that the phoneme was the invention of an individual, and ask what are the conditions that are likely to potentiate this invention. What must an individual recognize in order to consider that sounds need have no meaning, and thus that they could combine to form units that do have meaning? When each sound has only one meaning the sound—meaning relation is most likely to appear fixed. But when a stage is reached at which sounds have many meanings, recognition of the conventional character of the sound—meaning relation seems most likely to occur. If a sound can have arbitrarily many meanings — and meanings that are unrelated — then it can also have no meaning. I can do no more than suggest that the polysemous character of language was a precursor for the further recognition that sounds need have no meaning.

(Notice that phonetization, which preceded the syllabary and ultimately the alphabet, cannot occur until words have multiple meanings. This suggests, by a parallel argument, that the phoneme did not occur until words had at least some degree of multiple meanings, enough to potentiate the discovery.)

That the phoneme was a relatively late development is compatible with the argument that it represents a solution to the "large world" problem. Not until the world being mapped was relatively "large" would it seem likely that words would have multiple meanings.

References

Bandura, A. *Principles of behavior modification.* New York: Holt, 1969.
Durbin, M. Some non-arbitrary aspects of language. Paper presented at a meeting of the Anthropological Association, New York, 1971.
Gelb, I. J. *A study of writing.* Chicago, Illinois: Univ. of Chicago Press, 1963.
Goodall, J. Chimpanzees of the Gombi Stream Reserve. In I. Devore (Ed.), *Primate behavior.* New York: Holt, 1965.
Hewes, G. W. Primate communication and the gestural origin of language. *Current Anthropology* (in press).
Hockett, C. F. Animal "languages" and human language. *Human Biology*, 1959, 31, 32–39.
Köhler, W. *The mentality of apes.* New York: Harcourt, 1927.
Lubbock, J. Teaching animals to converse. *Nature*, 1884, 547–548.
Piaget, J., & Inhelder, B., *Mental imagery in the child.* New York: Basic Books, 1971.
Premack, D. Language in Chimpanzee? *Science*, 1971, 172, 808–822.
Reynolds, V., & Reynolds, F. Chimpanzees of the Budongo forest, In I. Devore (Ed.), *Primate behavior.* New York: Holt, 1965.
Wescott, R. Linguistic iconism. *Language*, 1971, 47, 416–428.

THE SIGNS OF LANGUAGE
IN CHILD AND CHIMPANZEE [1]

Edward S. Klima

Department of Linguistics
University of California at San Diego
La Jolla, California

Ursula Bellugi

The Salk Institute for Biological Studies
San Diego, California

The Signs of Language

Language can be investigated from several viewpoints. Of primary interest to many people is the way language functions as a means of communication. Others are interested in how language embodies thought or how it expresses feeling. Still others look at language as an aspect of social organization on the one hand, or of individual consciousness on the other. Students of literature are interested in language as the tool in the creative process of the verbal arts. There is also a small group of scholars obsessed with a very narrow, technical aspect of language – namely its *form*. Those scholars are now called *linguists,* and we are among them. But if the word "linguist" suggests a student of language in its most general sense, many of us would be happy to consider ourselves just plain grammarians, for like the ancient grammarians, we set as our goal the systematic description of the sounds, forms, syntax, and semantics of individual languages – i.e., particular grammars – and speculate about the traits common to all language – i.e., universal grammar. We also speculate about the historical aspect of language, both how its form is acquired by the child and how it changes over generations. We differ mostly from our predecessors in the explicitness we demand of our descriptions and in being primarily descriptive rather than prescriptive.

[1] This work was supported in part by NIH Grant NS 09811-01 to the Salk Institute and by NSF Grant GS-2982 to the University of California at San Diego.

In current usage, the word "language" is quite broad in its reference. Of course, it basically refers to the verbal language of man. We still use the phrase: "to speak a certain tongue"; and "language" has as its root the Latin word meaning "tongue." But we also speak of "the language of facial expression," "the language of the birds," "the language of art," "the language of love," even "the language of the gene," where "language" comes to mean simply the means by which information is communicated. These varied uses of the word "language" raise an interesting question; namely, do these other "languages" differ from verbal language only in the mode of expression, i.e., only in being other than vocal-auditory.

For a linguist, the observation that language is a symbolic system – like many other modes of communication – leads to a very crucial question: What is the nature of language symbolism? There are several ways, of course, of interpreting this question: One would be to ask for the necessary and sufficient conditions of linguistic symbolism. Here, however, we shall not be so ambitious as to ask what *must* occur in all languages but rather what *may* occur. That is, we ask merely, what is symptomatic of a language-like system in the behavior of its symbols. These symptoms need not necessarily occur in all human languages but, since we have every reason to think that at whatever the optimal language learning stage is any human being could learn any language, we assume these special character- istics – these possibilities – are part of our general linguistic competence.

Let us begin with some concrete examples at the most basic level of language symbolism – the word – often described as the minimal meaningful unit that may occur alone. And let us take for examples the words, *tape, take, lake, ought, awe,* and *raw.* These are symbols in the classical sense in having a meaning and a form, where the form is not predictable from the sense, i.e., where the physical characteristics of the form do not in some sense or other imitate aspects of the meaning. Now the form of these word symbols is constituted by one or more sound segments (or phonemes): in *raw* the *r*-sound followed by the *ô*-sound; in *paw* the *p*-sound followed by the *ô*-sound. These phonemes themselves do not carry any meaning but are just differential in their significance: *Paw* differs from *pa* in simply having an *ô*-sound after the *p*-sound rather than an *ä*-sound. One rash conclusion about the nature of language as a symbolic system that could be drawn from examples such as these is that a meaning is associated directly with a certain string of sounds. That the case is not so simple is indicated by the symbol which has as its form *awe* and its meaning "veneration." The sound has that meaning only if it is a word and not when it is a part of word as in *paw* and *raw*. The special feature of the form of language symbolism that this illustrates is the toleration of ambiguity – here, at the trivial level, a given form functions both as a meaningless formative and a meaningful symbol. And this ambiguity suggests the first level of abstraction in language: The sound form [ô] has the meaning "veneration" only if it is a word.

The case is even clearer with the meaningful units which do not occur alone: the so-called bound morphemes. The z-sound signifies plural in *pens* as opposed to *pen*. Here again the z-sound (that is, the form) when it occurs at the end of a symbol indicates plurality in items like *pens, bags,* etc. but not in *lens,* where the final z-sound is a meaningless part of the meaningful whole. In *laps*(e), we have a fully ambiguous form: on the one hand the plural of *lap*; on the other hand, a form meaning "passage" as in "a *lapse* of time." So again, this sort of ambiguity suggests that we have not only sound and meaning but abstract structure including morphemes: And the z-sound signifies plurality only when it is the realization of the abstract number morpheme.

Within the vocabulary of a language the presence (however exceptional) of homonyms represents a similar tolerance for ambiguity which suggests the operation of an abstract entity between form and meaning which we might call the lexeme. Take for example, the sound form [b-ĭ-l] (spelled *bill*) which has the dictionary meanings (1) an itemized account and (2) the beak of a bird, and contrast this form with *object* on the one hand and *parent* on the other. Now in referring to a restaurant bill and a bird's bill that are both lying on a table it is completely within proper usage to say that *two objects are on the table,* but certainly not *two bills are on the table,* which suggests that *bill* does not have a disjunction as its meaning, as one could conceive of in the case of the word *parent* (i.e., the *father* or *mother*) or *sibling* (i.e., *brother* or *sister*) but is rather the phonic realization of two different free morphemes. But once again this sort of reasoning involves an abstract notion of implicit structure (the morpheme), which is not shown in the physical form under consideration.

The phenomenon of ambiguity which we have been discussing is also found in syntax, where it became one of the main types of crucial examples invoked by transformationalists in demonstrating the abstractness of syntactic structure. Chomsky's (1957) ambiguous sentence: "Flying planes can be dangerous," will serve to illustrate the point. Here the ambiguity lies in the syntactic relation of the two elements in the phrase *flying planes,* where the forms are the same in both interpretations: the present participal form of the verb *fly* and the plural of the noun *planes,* and in both cases the phrase *flying planes* is subject of the sentence. But in its interpretation as an activity (*Flying these planes* can be dangerous), *planes* is a noun phrase object of *flying* and *flying planes* is a verb phrase, functioning as subject of *can be dangerous.* In the interpretation of *flying planes* as describing planes having the characteristic of flying (as in "*these flying planes* can be dangerous") *flying* itself is a verb phrase modifying the head noun *planes.* The phenomenon will be seen to be of the same general type as those ambiguities just discussed: again a single form (in this case the two-word phrase *flying planes*) is the realization of different abstract grammatical categories; that is, of grammatical categories which are not made explicit by a distinctive form.

So far, we have not referred to the *use* of these ambiguous forms — what they mean in actual discourse and how they are understood. A logical possibility in a symbolic system would be for such ambiguous expressions to include *both* meanings in a given sentence instance — as used in statements, for example — or to express uncertainty about which of the meanings is appropriate, and for the linguistic context to limit the meaning in certain cases. Thus, the statement *flying planes can be dangerous* in such a symbolic system would predicate *being dangerous* to both flying the planes and the planes themselves, whereas *flying planes is dangerous* would, by the linguistic context of the singular verb *is*, limit the meaning. But it is clear that in fact, this is not the nature of such ambiguous expressions in language. Rather, in a statement, they are used to mean either one or the other of their possible interpretations. That is, *planes* is either object of *flying* or *flying* is a modifier of planes in any one-sentence instance.

What then is the status of these ambiguities? The total effect is to make the language as a communicative device less than ideal. And we certainly do not maintain that they are a necessary characteristic of language. English would not be less language-like if it required an explicit form to mark the onset of an indefinite noun phrase like *planes* in the same way that English obligatorily marks the onset of definite noun phrases by *the, these, those,* etc. (*The flying planes can be dangerous. Flying the planes can be dangerous.*) Similarly, the language-like nature of English would not be affected if all root morphemes had the phonemic structure of a consonant followed by a vowel and all bound morphemes followed the root as vowel—consonant. On the other hand, when language has abstract grammatical categories like morpheme, word, noun, noun phrase, and clause, which are, as grammar shows, as real as the sounds of language, then one predicts the *possibility* of just such ambiguities as we have discussed. And conversely, the ways these ambiguities operate in human language, when they do occur, are very strong support for ascribing reality to such abstract categories. This is one aspect of the *abstractness* in the form of linguistic symbolism.

Structure and Well Formedness

The second aspect of linguistic symbolism we shall discuss is the extent to which it is a structured system: the extent to which each abstract linguistic category (word, phrase, sentence) is an integrated whole. As in the argument for the abstractness of grammar, we will present only symptoms of structure, and not necessarily structural characteristics that all human languages do or must have. By *integrated whole,* we mean such a unit whose constituents are so interrelated that one constituent may affect the form or occurrence of another constituent. Let us begin again at the level of the word (informally, one or more meaningful morphemes like *bake* and *baker*, where the morphemes themselves are represented by a string of meaningless, merely differential sound segments, i.e., phonemes). In many traditions, the word, or at least the word as a single free morpheme, has been viewed as the basic symbolic unit of language, since in no way could its constitutive sounds add up to its meaning. But there is also a certain type of relation between the sound segments in a word that is a symptom of its character as a unit, as an integrated whole. As an example, consider the following sound segments: the phonetically lax [ĕ], [ă], [ĭ], the phonetically tense [ä] and [ē] as they occur in *pet, pat, pit, pot, peat,* five different English words, which differ to the ear only in the quality of the vowel sound between the *p*-sound and the *t*-sound. Now it is, in fact, the case that there are actual words in English that end in the tense vowels [ä] and [ē], *pa,* and *ma, pea,* and *me*; it is also the case that there are no actual words that end in the lax vowels[2]; that is, there are no words like [pĕ] or [mĕ]; none like[pĭ] or [mĭ]; none like [pă] or [mă]. But of course in terms of actual English words while there is a word *pay,* there is no actual word *tay*; while there is a word *peat,* there is no actual word *reat*; while there is a word *paw,* there is no actual word *baw.* Yet somehow, *tay* and *reat* and *baw* are possible English words (i.e., they constitute a sound sequence that is wordlike) whereas [pă] and [rĕ] and [bĭ] are not only not actual words, they are not possible words in English. Indeed, in the dialect of English in question, there is a special *constraint* operative with lax vowels in general: They must be followed by a consonant. This is an instance of the interdependence of formal elements that is offered as a symptom of the word as a highly integrated whole. And typically, as in the case here, to say that words are tightly structured units is to say that there will be conditions on their well formedness, such that a certain combination of otherwise permissible constitutive elements (in this case sound segments) while similar to segments occurring in actual words, may simply not qualify as a possible word. At the syntactic level, where the meanings of the individual words are associated with one another in sentences, there have been two radically opposed notions of the nature of this relationship. Certain students of language, and particularly psychologists of language, have treated the relationship between the main constitutive elements of the sentence as being very loose, the meanings of the individual constituents of the sentence interacting with one another in certain more or less favored ways, with the result a composite sentential meaning richer than those of the individual symbols. So in *hunters kill animals* the process would be no different in principle from that relating the components of a string like: *the hunters – the*

---

[2] We shall exclude, for the purpose of this discussion, the onomatopoetic sheep call *baa* when pronounced [bă], as well as the interjection *yeah!* [yă] (yes). It is not unusual for the interjections used by a particular speech community to include sounds that lie outside of the phonological structure of the language itself. We shall also not comment further on the quality of the final vowel sound of the unaccented syllable of *city, party.*

animals – the kill. Linguists working in syntax, on the other hand, have presented very strong reasons for concluding that sentences are indeed not at all like phrases of the type *the hunters – the animals – the kill,* that sentences are very tightly structured units of a hierarchic nature. The current linguistic literature is rich with discussions about the nature of syntactic structure and the sort of formal devices that are adequate for describing the syntax of natural languages. Here, however, we shall limit ourselves to a very informal discussion of phenomena which are indicative of the reality of the sentence as a highly integrated, tightly structured whole. Let us consider certain very simple sentences of the type *hunters kill animals.*

(1) *Somebody sang something somewhere.*
(2) *Somebody made something somewhere.*
(3) *Somebody put something somewhere.*

To facilitate discussion, we shall call such simple sentences *simple propositional phrases,* thus contrasting them with sentences like "The man who called thought you returned." We shall consider the latter a *complex propositional phrase,* consisting of a composite of simple propositional phrases, approximately "The man called," "The man thought so," and "You returned."

In Sentences 1–3, *someone, something,* and *somewhere* are, of course, particular representatives of subject nominal, object nominal, and locational nominal. Superficially, the sentences are the same in their form except for the difference in the verb, and since *someone, something,* and *somewhere* are representative of indefinitely many different forms of subject, object, and location, we are dealing not with three sentences but indefinitely many. There are some interesting differences however, in how these strings of four words behave. Sentences representing a simple propositional phrase like (1) with the verb *sing* need *not* express in words either the object or the location; i.e., "Somebody sang" is well formed, as is "Somebody sang something," and "Somebody sang somewhere." Simple propositional phrase sentences like (2) with the verbs *make* are well formed without the location expressed in words but are not well formed (i.e., not grammatical) if the object is *not* explicitly specified by some word or phrase, i.e., *Somebody made* is not a well-formed sentence and neither is *Somebody made somewhere.* In sentences representing simple propositions like (3) with the verb *put,* both the object and location must be included explicitly as a linguistic form, i.e., all of the following are ungrammatical: *Somebody put something, Somebody put somewhere, Somebody put.* What is significant here is that appropriate linguistic *forms* must accompany *put* (object and location) and *make* (object) and that this formal constraint holds, no matter how indefinite a notion of *putting* or *making* is involved and no matter how clear the context. Here we have a syntactic constraint with certain similarities to the phonological phenomenon discussed above. In this case, the class of verb puts certain constraints on the phrases that accompany it in the simple propositional phrase.

Now consider the following sentences with the same verbs *make* and *put*.

(4) These things are going to be hard for you to *make*.
(5) These things are going to be hard for you to *put* in that box.

The two sentences reflect a similar alignment of constituents – a subject (*these things*), a predicate agreeing in number with its subject (*are going to be hard*) followed by a qualifying phrase (*for you to make* and *to put in that box*). It would appear then that the constraint observed with verbs like *put* and *make* in simple propositonal phrases (namely, that they must have an explicit grammatical object) is relaxed in these complex propositional phrases.[3] But on closer examination we discover that this is not the case. In fact, in these constructions it is not only the case that *put* and *make need* not have a grammatical object but they *must* not; and while the nominal *these things* is indeed the grammatical subject of the predicate *are hard,* it is at the same time *understood* unambiguously as also functioning as the object of *make* and *put*.[4] Thus we see that very rigid constraints of a purely formal nature operate not only within a simple proposition but also across propositions.

We began with the traditional notion of the word as the basic unit in language symbolism. We then developed the argument that the sentence, like the word, involves abstract unspoken categories and manifests the presence of a tight structure formally even more complex in the interdependencies among its components than the structure of the word. Moreover, a sentence as a whole has a meaning that does not just represent the sum of the meanings of the words that, in the form of sound, represent its physical realization. To demonstrate this we need only recall the phrase: *the hunters – the animals – the kill.* While that phrase may *suggest* that the hunters killed the animals, the sentence "The hunters killed the animals" does more than suggest it, the sentence indeed means that the hunters killed the animals, much in the same way as the riddle: "It's black and white and re(a)d all over" may *suggest* a daily publication on folded paper, whereas the word newspaper *means* a daily publication on folded paper.

We see then that the sentence is *not* a mere collection of symbols like the

[3] The complex propositional phrases illustrated by Sentences (4) and (5) can be thought of as representing the combining of the simple propositional phrase *it is hard* with one or the other of these simple propositional phrases: *for you to make these things* or *for you to put these things in that box.*

[4] In the current transformational analysis of such sentences, from a structure something like *It is going to be hard to make these things,* the grammatical object (*these things*) leaves its subordinate propositional phrase and replaces the subject *it* of the superordinate propositional phrase (*it is hard*).

phrase *the hunters – the animals – the kill* but is indeed itself a complex symbol.

Language Experiments with Chimpanzees

It is generally accepted that human beings are the only animals that develop speech as a natural part of their ordinary social maturation. And many would conclude, from this observation, that only human beings have the potential for language – i.e., for the type of symbolic system that language represents. Indeed, dismal failure has been the outcome of all attempts to teach animals to speak or to provide them with an environment sufficiently enriched with speech to permit them to learn to speak. Our evolutionarily close relatives, the chimpanzees, have been subjects of several such experiments in the past 40 years. The Kelloggs (Kellogg & Kellogg, 1933; Kellogg, 1968) raised the female infant chimp Gua with their own son Donald, who was about the same age. In the 9 months of the experiment, Gua did not learn to speak a single word, but did learn to respond to more than 60 different English sentences. Later Keith and Cathy Hayes (Hayes, 1951; Hayes, 1951) adopted Viki, a 3-day old female chimpanzee. They worked with her intensively for 6½ years. Viki learned to make four sounds that were sometimes recognizable as English words, associated with four individual objects. The sounds were learned only with the greatest difficulty. The Hayes had to shape Viki's mouth with their hands and induce her to try shaping it with her own hands. Even then there were confusions and inappropriate uses.

These experiences make it seem that a vocal language is not appropriate for a chimpanzee. We know that there are distinct differences between the articulatory apparatus of the nonhuman primates and that of man, most recently from the work of Philip Lieberman (1968) at Haskins Laboratory. Lieberman argued that the vocal mechanisms of nonhuman primates are not capable of producing human speech sounds. This is a result of an anatomical lack of tongue mobility, among other things. It seems that nonhuman primates cannot change the shape of their vocal tract to control the necessary variety of sounds, the way human beings can for the thousands of languages of the world.

The next step that obviously had to be taken in these experiments was to explore the chimpanzee's ability in language-like behavior in some mode in which, unlike vocalization, the chimpanzee could easily operate. Within the past 5 years, there have been two extremely interesting experiments along these lines. One of these experiments was carried out by the Gardners, two psychologists at the University of Nevada (Gardner & Gardner, 1969). They reasoned that while the chimpanzee might well be incapable of vocalization, its behavior in the wild suggests that it was very adroit indeed in the control of its manual gestures. To ensure that the manual system would in fact not be based on spoken language and yet would be actually used by human beings, they cleverly chose the sign language of the deaf in America.

The other very significant experiment is still being conducted. David Premack (1971) of the University of California at Santa Barbara similarly chose to free the chimpanzee of whatever limitation in language-like communication its difficulty in vocalization might present. He provided the chimpanzee with ready-made tokens of varying shape, size, and color for use as wordlike units, and provided it with a magnetic board as the channel, i.e., on which the tokens could be arranged in sequences by or for the chimpanzee. In both of these recent experiments, the question is: What aspects of human language will a higher animal learn under conditions of extended exposure to a language, or even when subjected to intensive training. This, of course, is not a question of the animal's *natural* behavior in its natural environment but rather a question of its capabilities in an environment that is manipulated in various *unnatural* ways.

The early results of the two experiments are now readily accessible in nontechnical terms (Gardner & Gardner, 1969; Premack, 1971). In brief, the Gardners obtained a chimpanzee (Washoe) from the wild in June 1966, when she was about 1 year old. Striving to make a rich homelike atmosphere for the chimpanzee (*homelike* in terms of a human child's home), the Gardners signed to her in sentences as they prepared her meals, dressed her, and played with her in much the same way as parents chatter with their children. In their signed sentences they tried to follow the word order of English. In the sessions devoted explicitly to training, during the early part of the experiment, the Gardners specifically trained Washoe to make individual signs. By comparison with the four words that Viki learned to speak, Washoe's progress in the production of signs seems spectacular indeed. By about 4 years old she had already learned to make reliably more than 80 different signs.

It seems clear from this experiment that Washoe not only has learned to make manual gestures, but makes them in ways that clearly refer to aspects of her external environment. Her ability to name shows a development that in many respects is similar to that of a young child. She first learned the sign for *open* with a particular door. She then extended the use of that sign far beyond the original training, first to all closed doors, then to closed containers such as the refrigerator, cupboards, drawers, briefcases, boxes, and jars. Eventually she spontaneously used the sign for *open* to request opening of the water faucet and of a closed bottle of soda pop. She learned a sign for *cat* and a sign for *dog*, originally primarily with pictures of each, and she uses the signs appropriately while looking through magazines or books as well as for real cats and dogs. She made the sign for *dog* even when someone drew a caricature of a dog for her, and also when she heard a dog that she could not see barking in the distance.

At first, Washoe used signs singly like *open* and *more*. Then as soon as she knew 8 or 10 signs the Gardners report she began using combinations of signs in sequences, and by the time she was 4 years old, there were sometimes three or more signs in a sequence. The Gardners recorded all new combinations that they had observed Washoe making, and by the end of 14 months after her first signed combination, they had recorded 330 different combinations of signs. We have the same sort of information for one hearing child, Gregory, provided by the psychologist Martin Braine (1963). Gregory first produced an utterance which combined two words when he was 19 months old, and his parents recorded all new combinations thereafter. Seven months later, he had produced more than 2500 different combinations; his parents could no longer reasonably keep track. Certainly there is an enormous difference in sheer productivity, but the crucial differences are more profound than this.

A good example of Washoe's combinations involves the sign for *open* which was one of the first Washoe learned to use, and she used it frequently. When she had learned other signs, she eventually began combining them with *open,* and produced the following sequences, for example:

open out	(when standing in front of a trailer door)
open flower	(to be let through the gate to the flower garden)
food open hurry	(at the refrigerator door)
key open please blanket	(at the bedding cupboard)
open key clean	(at the soap cupboard)

These are all appropriate combinations, relevant to a particular context; some may not be copies of sentences she has seen other people sign, that is, may be original for Washoe. She does produce names that are fitting to a particular situation, and she combines them in sequences — spontaneously.

The Gardners report, that for many combinations, all orders have occurred at least once. For example, she has produced *open drink* and *drink open; key open* and *open key; more open* and *open more*; the three sign sequence: *please sweet drink* has been produced in all possible orders. However, there may indeed be certain preferential orders — the Gardners have not yet reported on this. It seems to us, though, that Washoe's meager production of combinations and her freedom with sign order should not be allowed to result in overhasty conclusions about limitations in what she has the ability to communicate. Washoe's impressive performance in learning to assign names to things, or classes of things comes as a result of specific training designed to teach her that very task. It should be remembered that Washoe did not naturally start signing in the way that children start phonating (or indeed as the children of the deaf start signing). She was induced to make signs, by reward, by modeling, etc. The Gardners' experiment suggests that a chimpanzee can be taught selective elements of a manual language and can use these productively, for novel instances, when these elements correspond to individual wordlike elements — the sign for *flower,* for *tickling,* for *cat.* That Washoe did not spontaneously capture the relationships implicit between the signs in the sentences to which she was exposed should not be surprising. What was demonstrated with Washoe's impressive naming was that she could be taught to associate a visual–manual token with objects or events, and then was able to generalize the use of the token to similar objects and events, though, of course, we do not know by precisely what criterion of similarity.

The reason for the interest in Washoe's multisign message formations is that this is the context in which the differing roles of the various signs are specified with respect to the total picture. It seems clear that Washoe can be taught to perform simple naming; her own behavior indicates that she can similarly perform complex naming, emit a string of tokens jointly associated with a situation. It is quite another question whether she can be taught to distinguish in the *form* of the message between such differing relations as actor versus acted on – the sort of thing which some languages (like English) accomplish with word order in differentiating *John tickles Mary* from *Mary tickles John,* and which other languages accomplish with different formal devices.

In terms of the formal characteristics of the symbolic system of human language discussed in the first section of this paper, naturally there are far too few data from the Gardner experiment to draw any conclusions. And of course from the viewpoint of Professor Premack's (1971) experiment, new testing routines would have to be devised to determine whether the tolerance for ambiguities, for example, or the complex interdependencies could be trained in the chimpanzee. We again stress that these need not be *necessary* characteristics of some particular human language, but that they must certainly be *possible* characteristics. As such they are obviously included in the competence for language.

Language in a Different Mode

The Gardner experiment in particular, which was intentionally modeled after a real form of human communication (but one circumventing the limitations in chimpanzee vocalization) raises interesting questions beyond mere speculation about whether Washoe's signing is a "language" in the sense of a human language. One question it raises has to do with the nature of human gestural language itself. The question is fundamental: When the *primary* mode of language communication is visual–gestural rather than acoustic–articulatory, does this difference in mode affect in any substantial way the characteristics of the system as a language? Are there special formal structural characteristics associated with the manual–visual mode?

Of course, in a general sense of "communicate," we all use the visual mode for communicating certain things. The face can be used in very subtle ways to communicate, as can the hands, the head, the whole body in its many expressive postures. But in the ordinary speaking–hearing world, the primary mode of asserting, for predicating, for "propositionalizing" is the speech mode, although, of course, the message may be transformed *derivatively* into a visual form as in writing and semaphore. For the congenitally deaf, however, the situation is quite different — and, of course, quite complex.

Let us consider first the total picture of language communication among the profoundly deaf. There are at least three different varieties of manual language among the deaf. One is based entirely on written English; it uses the visual mode, but is derivative, in much the same way as written language: It is quite appropriately called *fingerspelling.* There is a hand alphabet in which each letter of the English alphabet is represented by a different hand configuration, and each English word is simply written in the air. The second variety of manual language uses a combination of fingerspelling and signs, but stays as close as possible to written English in word order and morphology. This is called *Signed English,* and is used primarily in instruction and in formal situations. The third type of manual language is the one we will be concerned with here, sometimes called *American Sign Language of the Deaf.* It is the language the deaf use among themselves when they communicate, and ordinarily it is the language that the deaf child learns from his deaf parents. It is not a derivative language in the sense of the other two. It has its own syntax, its own processes of word formation, and its own methods of incorporating semantic variation into its basic units: the sign and the sign phrase. Certain aspects of American Sign Language are shared with spoken language; others seem to be quite unique, ascribable perhaps to the visual–manual mode itself. These similarities and differences will be discussed in the following sections. American Sign Language is geographically determined, as is any other language: For example, the sign language developed in Great Britain is totally different from that used in America. Each sign language is essentially an abstract system and not a more or less universally understood pantomime (although in longer narrative, the deaf do use pantomime as a supplement to sign language).

The different renderings of the following passage will give some idea of the differences involved in the three varieties of manual language used by the American deaf. The example is taken from a longer passage in some memory experiments we have been conducting. (A hyphen between letters indicates fingerspelling. A word in capital letters represents a sign of American Sign Language presented in its approximate English equivalent. A + between English glosses represents semantically distinct parts of a single sign.)

Fingerspelling

H-e   w-o-u-l-d   g-i-v-e   h-i-s   d-a-u-g-h-t-e-r   t-h-e   b-e-s-t   f-i-s-h   a-n-d
t-h-e   v-i-l-l-a-g-e-r-s   w-o-u-l-d   b-u-y   t-h-e   r-e-s-t   f-r-o-m   h-i-m.

Signed English

> H-E THINK PAST H-E W-D [for "would"] KEEP BEST FISH FOR H-S [for "his"] DAUGHTER AND LEFT, H-E W-D SELL TO PEOPLE IN THAT TOWN [with "v" hand configuration].

American Sign Language

> THINK. "ME COLLECT FISH, BIG+PILE FISH. BEST PICK GIVE DAUGHTER." THINK. "BEST GIVE+HER. ME TOWN SELL EARN MONEY." THINK.

As can be seen from this example, American Sign Language is not just signed English. And while it is possible to give an English gloss to signs, there is no one-to-one correspondence between sign and English word. American Sign Language characteristically does not include the copula, the auxiliary *do* or *be*, articles, or most suffixes and prefixes. It must be constantly remembered that sign is expressed in physical gestures that take place in the space between the signer and addressee, and that aspects of the modality itself shape and constrain the language.

The Sign Itself

Each sign can be described according to three parameters which occur simultaneously: (a) the *hand configuration* involved in the sign; (b) the *place* in relation to the body where the sign is made; and (c) *movement* of the sign. For example, in making the sign glossed as the interrogative WHAT the signing hand has the configuration of index finger extended from fist. The tip of the index finger contacts the open palm of the other hand, palm up. The fingertip moves across the palm of the hand toward the signer. If instead, the open hand is held palm down and the side of the index finger of the other hand grazes against the palm away from the signer, the sign means KILL (Stokoe, 1960; Stokoe, Casterline, & Croneberg, 1965).

While the three parameters may be combined abstractly to form a single sign, there are families of semantically related signs that use elements of the same parameter in a systematic way. We shall describe families of signs which are related in terms of hand configuration, place of articulation, and direction of movement.

Hand Configuration

There are a number of signs which share a particular hand configuration, although the location of the sign in relation to the body and the movement is different for each of the signs. These signs sometimes have a common semantic component of emotion or feeling: HEART, TERRIBLE, HATE, FEEL, SICK,

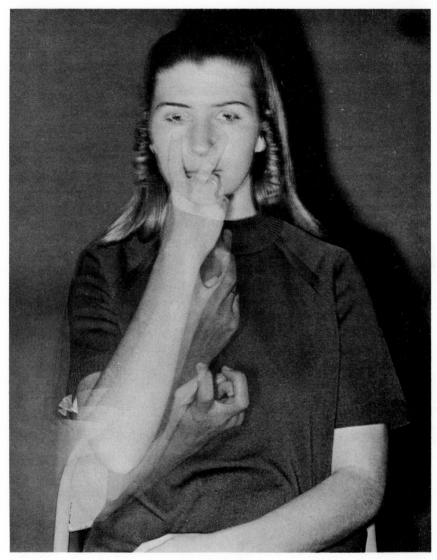

Fig. 1. DOUBT.

EXCITED, DELICIOUS, PITY, DISCOURAGED. In forming these signs, the hand configuration involves the middle finger bent slightly forward from a flat hand with the fingers spread out. Other signs which use the same hand shape do not have the same semantic value, for example: TELEGRAM or BARE.

To consider another example, there are signs that share a different hand shape – the index finger and middle finger are extended outward from a fist;

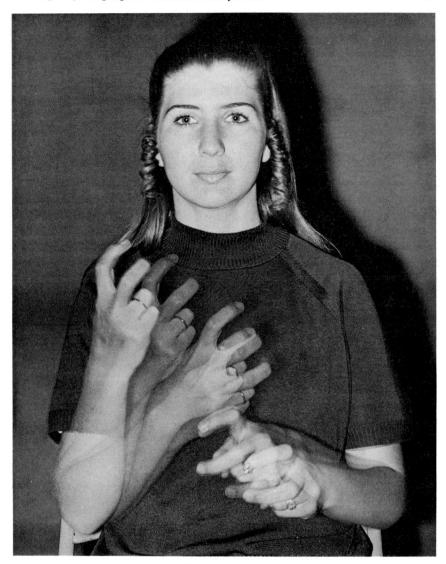

Fig. 2. HARD.

they are spread apart and bent at the knuckles. This handshape is the configurational parameter of signs like SQUIRREL or POTATO, where it is purely formative, but is also a shared component of signs which have common semantic value (roughly, of "negative evaluation") for example, DIFFICULTY, PROBLEM, STEAL, SELFISH, STRICT, LIPREADING, DOUBT, and HARD (Figs. 1 and 2).

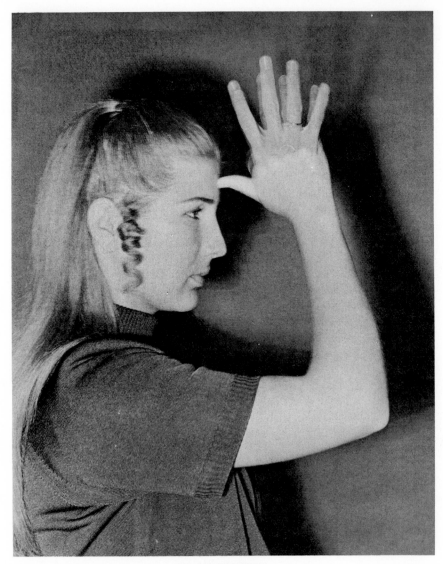

Fig. 3. FATHER.

Place of Articulation

There is a family of sign pairs (FATHER–MOTHER (Figs. 3 and 4), BOY–GIRL, GRANDFATHER–GRANDMOTHER, BROTHER–SISTER, HUSBAND–WIFE, SON–DAUGHTER, UNCLE–AUNT) in which the only difference within each pair is the place of articulation (forehead versus lower

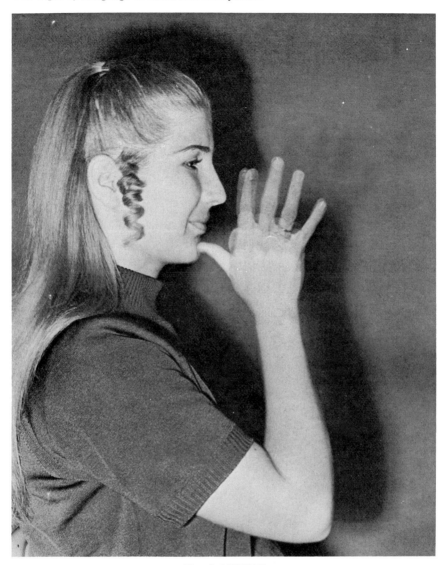

Fig. 4. MOTHER.

cheek). The same difference is common to the whole family and clearly has the semantic value of male versus female. However, other signs with the same locational parameters like PENNY (on forehead) or CANDY (on lower cheek) do not have a semantic value associated with that parameter. Thus, a locational feature that is semantic in one sign may be merely formative in another – as is the case in the sound segments of spoken of spoken language.

Fig. 5. KNOW.

Movement

Signs take place in the physical space in front of the signer's body between signer and addressee. The use of space, direction, and movement, are all crucial in sign language, and give it quite a different character from spoken language. Signs may be made with one or both hands, or occasionally even two different

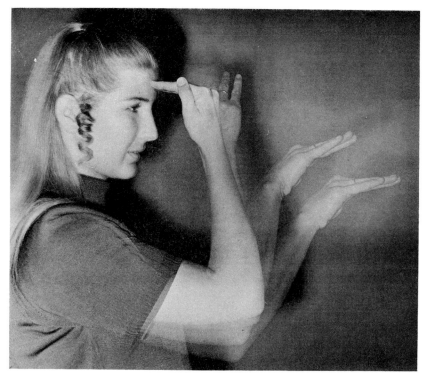

Fig. 6. DON'T+KNOW.

signs may be made simultaneously. The use of space in front of the signer can be an indicator for intonational cues in an utterance. When viewed under slow motion, we see that a signer's hands often come to a rest in front of the body at the end of a sentence, and that questions may be marked by the hands pausing almost imperceptibly or moving slightly toward the addressee (see Stokoe *et al.,* 1965.

Signers often use the space in front of their bodies to locate objects, persons, the subject of their discourse, and (perhaps because our memory for spatial arrangements is so well developed) they can then continue to refer to these topics in the allocated space or direction. Let us consider a few of the specific ways in which movement is used as a parameter of signing.

There is a family of sign pairs which share the same hand configuration and place of articulation in relation to the body. They differ only in that the motion involved is in opposite directions. Among these pairs are JOIN–DISCONNECT; THRILLED–DISCOURAGED; APPEAR–DISAPPEAR; TAKE+UP–DROP; WITH–WITHOUT.

Some signs have a lexical negation which is missing in the corresponding

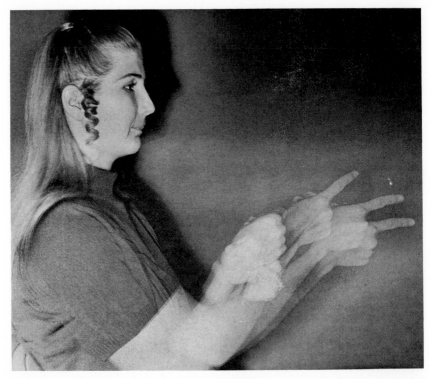

Fig. 7. NEXT+YEAR.

English word. The sign for KNOW (Fig. 5) is a bent hand, fingers together, in which the fingertips come to touch the forehead. The sign for DON'T+KNOW (Fig. 6) is the same handshape which touches the forehead and then the fingertips move away from the signer (the wrist turns) and the hand moves slightly downward and away from the signer. The signs for DON'T+CARE, DON'T+WANT, and BAD all share the same downward movement away from the signer. Again, not all signs which share the same hand motion have a negative meaning, however. In the sign for TASTY, the movement of turning the hand away from the signer and moving slightly downward is a formative without negative semantic value. The sign for LOOK+AT begins with a handshape that touches the face under the eyes. The hand then moves away from the signer and usually downward, but it has no negative value.

Many signs that indicate past and future share a common direction of movement. Signs that indicate the future move forward from the signer. Signs which indicate the past generally move toward the signer and over the shoulder. Thus the sign which is glossed WILL or IN+THE+FUTURE moves from the cheek in a forward arc. The sign which is glossed PAST moves toward the

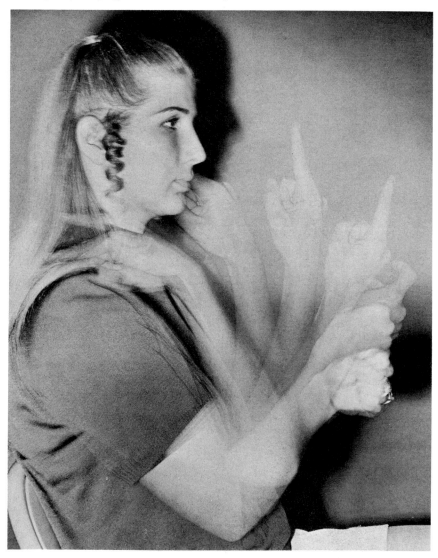

Fig. 8. LAST+YEAR.

signer's shoulder in the reverse direction. Other pairs include NEXT+YEAR–LAST+YEAR (Figs. 7 and 8), NEXT+WEEK–LAST+WEEK; TOMORROW–YESTERDAY. The verbal sign for LOOK can be modified within these parameters. Moving the sign in a forward arc can mean PROPHECY. Making the sign in an arc which faces the signer and moves back across the region of the ear can mean REMINISCING. Another modification of the basic sign for LOOK

Fig. 9. I+INFORM+YOU.

which moves forward away from the signer can mean TO+LOOK+ANGRILY rather than to look forward, so these movements are sometimes an arbitrary part of the sign, rather than part of a semantic family of signs.

Another use of motion differentiates collective from singular instances. Thus, TREE may be designated by one motion of the wrist while the forearm remains in one location. To sign FOREST a signer may use the same handshape and position, but repeat the wrist motion several times while varying slightly the position of the forearm. Still another use of motion may distinguish aspects of verbal notions. A tapered hand with the thumb and fingertips touching which contacts the mouth is the sign for EAT. The same handshape with a repetitive circular motion which approaches the mouth means CONTINUALLY+EATING. To sign "He invited me," a signer may make the sign for INVITE once. To sign "Many people invited me," the sign for INVITE may be repeated several times in slightly different locations, and so forth.

A crucial use of movement, space, and direction is in the incorporation of subject or object in a verbal notion or sign. Since signs are made spatially between signer and addressee, direction of movement is often used to indicate the subject and/or object of a verbal notion. As an example, the signs which are

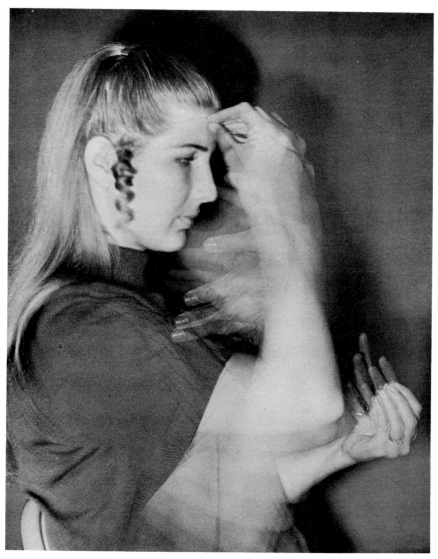

Fig. 10. YOU+INFORM+ME.

glossed I+INFORM+YOU and YOU+INFORM+ME can each be made as single unambiguous signs which are the same in hand configuration and place of articulation, but the direction of motion changes (Figs. 9 and 10). The third person is usually designated by similar spatial locations (the place the person was last seen, a line of sight diagonal to the signer and addressee, or the previous establishment in space of a person or thing). A large number of signs may change direction to incorporate subject or object: among them TEACH, COPY, INVITE, GIVE, ASK, HELP, LOOK+AT, and SEND. Although the class of verbal signs that may be reversed in direction seems to be large, it does not include all verbal signs. It may be that the class of verbs which do not change is as unpredictable as English irregular verbs or nouns. It may also be that these nonchanging verbs are different in some other respects. Among those that do not change in the paradigm "I do something to you." "You do something to me" are CHASE, FOLLOW, WANT, LEAD, REQUEST, and FIRE.

As should be clear from the examples above, American Sign Language uses aspects of the three formational parameters in very productive ways to express semantic variations in individual signs: Families of semantically related signs share one or more formational parameters; deictic and temporal concepts are incorporated into the sign. These are roughly equivalent to derivational morphology in spoken languages, although in American Sign Language there is special use of the spatial properties of the manual–visual mode. On the other hand, relational or functional morphology is not at all developed in American Sign Language: The form of the sign itself does not indicate such functions as subject of a verb versus object of the verb. That is, there is no general sign equivalent to the abstract linguistic notion of grammatical case; nor is there any formal device to mark agreement between modifier and modified. In this respect, American Sign Language is similar to English. Moreover, there is no formal agreement, in number or person, between the subject and the predicate.

Despite the absence of relational morphology, American Sign Language has relatively free word order within the basic phrases: Within the noun phrase, modifying adjectives may occur before and/or after the modified noun; subject noun phrase, object noun phrase, and main verb are freer in their order of occurrence than in English, for example. (Although the details of the values of the varying orders remain to be specified, concepts like topic and focus are clearly involved.)

In American Sign Language, when a particular nominal term in a construction is clear from the linguistic context (e.g., when the reference has already been specified by an explicit noun phrase), then the term is simply left unexpressed. That is, where some languages, like English, realize such a term as a pronoun, American Sign Language may omit the expression altogether.

Preliminary Experimental Data: Memory Tests

From some preliminary tests of short-term memory with the congenitally deaf, it seems that memory and storage are influenced by the parameters we have been describing. In remembering unrelated words, the most frequent incorrect responses made by hearing people involve words that have a phonological resemblance to the word they originally heard. In the studies we have begun with the deaf, signs were presented on videotape, and the individual's responses in signs were videotaped.[5] The most frequent incorrect responses were signs which shared most of the formal properties of the sign that had been presented, but perhaps differed from it in one of the major parameters.

(a) As an example, a sign that was perceived as TIME was remembered as POTATO: The place of articulation and movement of the two are almost the same, and the signs differ only in that one has a hand configuration which uses one finger and the other uses two fingers. The same relation holds for BIRD and DUCK.

(b) A sign that was perceived as VOTE was remembered as TEA. The hand configuration and place of articulation of the two signs is the same; they differ only slightly in movement, since one uses a single definite motion and the other a small circle of movement. CHURCH was remembered as CHOCOLATE, and the same relation holds between the two.

(c) A sign that was perceived as STAR was remembered as SOCKS. The hand configuration and direction of movement of the two signs are the same. The difference is in the place of articulation: one is made on the inside of the wrist and one on the outside of the wrist. APPLE was remembered as ONION. The signs differ only in place of articulation: One is on the cheek and the other on the temple.

Observations on Sign as a First Language

How is this language acquired in the relatively rare case of a deaf child of deaf parents? We find, on all counts that we can measure (except perhaps the amount of signing in an hour's time) that the language acquisition process proceeds in a very natural way precisely on schedule, when compared with the hearing children we have studied. We have tapes of an 18-month-old child whose vocabulary is well over 50 different signs. And we have monthly videotapes of mother—child interaction in sign over a period of 18 months, starting with another child, Pola, when she was 2 years and 7 months old. All the interaction takes place in sign language.

Although we are only beginning the kind of analysis we want to make of the child's language, some developments already seem clear. For the most part, her parents did not correct her arrangements of sequences of signs, her repetitions, her overgeneralizations of patterns in sign language. We look for the occurrence, nonoccurrence, and systematic overgeneralizations the child makes within these patterns. First, let us consider the schedule of language develop-

---

[5] At the conclusion of the tests, the deaf person himself and an independent judge gave English glosses to the signs.

ment. Considering the difference in modality, we might ask whether or not we might expect to find the same kinds of milestones, the same type of development as in hearing children.

In studies with hearing children, Brown, Cazden and Bellugi (1969) found a considerable range in the age at which they began to produce utterances of more than one word and some differences in the rate of progress, as measured by the appearance of certain types of constructions. What was strikingly similar was the order of emergence of constructions across children. Perhaps one could make an analogy with the emergence of teeth; there is in general a regular order but the ages and age ranges may differ for the appearance of particular teeth. Rather than use age as a general guideline for comparing children, then, we chose another measure – the mean utterance length (m.u.l.) in morphemes, which tended to increase in a sharp steady rise over time. New developments in the child's grammar were reflected in that increase. Furthermore, at various m.u.l. points we found striking commonalities in the details of development among hearing children. At first this was based on the incidence from three unacquainted children, Adam, Eve, and Sarah, studied by Roger Brown and a group of his colleagues at Harvard (see Brown, 1970). Since then, evidence has been collected from a number of other sources to add to that – children learning American English in other parts of the country, children learning Finnish, Samoan, Luo, and Japanese. Although all the evidence is not yet all in, it seems that there are some very important commonalities across children and across languages (Slobin, 1971).

With this as a background, we can examine the early material from language acquisition of one deaf child of deaf parents, Pola. There are many problems with calculating the mean utterance length in signs as compared with morphemes for spoken words. We decided to count morphemes for spoken English and not to count immediate repetitions in sign, thus giving an advantage to spoken English. Even so, the results shown in Table 1 demonstrate that a deaf child's

TABLE 1

Mean Utterance Length in Signs[a]

Pola's age	Videotape number	Mean utterance length
2.7	I	1.69
2.8	II	1.83
2.9	III	2.20
2.10	IV	2.32
2.11	V	2.36
3.0	VI	2.79

[a]Count is based on 200 consecutive utterances from hour-length videotape sessions. Does not include immediate repetition of signs.

m.u.l. in signs increased dramatically from the first month of our study as did that of hearing children. At 2 years and 7 months it was about 1.7 signs per utterance. Five months later it was about 2.8 signs per utterance. When we compared the child's progress with that of the three children studied by the Harvard group, we found that her development is entirely comparable with the hearing children.

When we examine some of the deaf child's typical signed sentences at what is comparable to Stage I, we find that her sequences fall into the same range of sentence functions and semantic relations (although there is less reliance on order to express these relations) (see Table 2). What of her vocabulary in signs? It seems to cover the full range of concepts expressed by hearing children of a comparable age. Among the signs she uses spontaneously are NAME, STAY, FINISH, WILL, TOMORROW, MORNING, MORE, WHAT, WHERE, WHO, WHY, HOW, FINGERSPELL, DEAD, KNOW, UNDERSTAND, FIVE, FOUR, TWO, THREE, and the letters of the alphabet. (See Table 3 for a partial listing of her vocabulary.)

Perhaps the most interesting and provocative finding to date is the evidence (slight to begin with) of overgeneralization on the part of the child learning sign as a native language. We have described the common morphological property of some negative signs (DON'T+KNOW, DON'T+WANT, BAD). These share in common a positioning of the hand face downward and a movement downward and away from signer. For the first 4 months of our study the child used only two rather primitive negative indications – a negative head shake and another

Table 2
Semantic Relations Sign Language

Pola, 2.7–2.8 Years

I. *Genitive and attribute*
(That) pink. (That) purple. (That) green. Many candy.
Many light (there). (That) dirty. (Me) napkin. (That) clean.

II. *Agent, action, and object*
Man work. Daddy shave. Man drive. Duck eat . . . grab.
Grab boy. Duck grab. Boy hit boy.

III. *Affected person, state, and object*
Want napkin. Want open. (Me) want (that). (Me) angry.
(You) angry. Ursula look (that).

IV. *Locative*
Letty (me) school. (Me) go home. Letty come home, school.

V. *Dative*
Give+(me) (that). (That) give+(her). Give+(me) orange.
(You)+give+(her).

TABLE 3
Pola's Vocabulary in Signs (Ages 2.7–3.0)

Proper nouns
  Aunt, Daddy, Darlene, Don, Grace, Grandmother, Letty, Mommy, Pola, Rick, Santa, Sheila, Tom, Ursula

Animate nouns (including animals)
  baby, bear, bird, boy, butterfly, cameraman, cat, clown, cow, crocodile, deer, doctor, dog, duck, elephant, frog, giraffe, girl, goat, hippo, horse, insect, lion, man, monkey, mouse, pig, rabbit, rhino, rooster, sheep, turtle, woman

Edible nouns
  apple, birthday+cake, bread, butter, cake, candy, cheese, chocolate, cookie, crackers, drink, egg, fish, gum, ice+cream, lettuce, milk, peanut, potato, raisin, sandwich, water

Other nominals
  arm, ball, baseball+bat, bath, beard, birthday, boat, book, brush, camera, car, chair, clothes, color, comb, cup, doll, dry, earring, fire, flower, fork, gun, hair, hanger, hankie, hearing+aid, helmet, home, house, knife, letter, light, lipstick, marble, mask, money, mouth, movie, name, napkin, necklace, nose, ocean, party, pants, picture, pipe, pitchfork, purse, rag, sandals, school, shoe, soap, spoon, stethoscope, switch, table, tooth, telephone, TV, toothpaste, t-o-y-s, train, trash, umbrella, volley+ball, water, watch, window

Modifiers
  angry, big, black, blue, brown, clean, dead, dirty, dumb, fat, five, four, full, funny, good, green, grey, hard, hot, hungry, many, maybe, melt, more, new, old, one, orange, pink, pretty, purple, red, silly, sticky, small, sweet, three, two, wet, wide, white, yellow

Temporal
  stay, will, tomorrow, morning, finish

Negatives
  no, n-o, not, can't, don't+want, don't+know, neg, none, nothing

Questions
  question+sign, what, where, who, why, how

Verbals
  ask, bite, blow, blot, bring, break, come, come+here, come+on, come+over, cook, cry, cut, cut+hair, draw, eat, enjoy, erase, fall, fall+off, fall+down, fingerspell, fight, fix, fix+hair, fly, give, go, gone, grab, have, hear, hit, hug, hunt, know, laugh, leave, lick, like, look, make, move, open, peel, pick+up, play, potty, pour, press+on, push+in, put+in, put+down, read, see, sew, shake, shave, sit, sleep, spank, spell, spill, squeeze, swim, take, take+off, talk, tell, throw, throw+away, touch, turn+on, turn+over, understand, wait, wake+up, walk, want, wash, wash+face, wipe+up, work, write

Prepositional (see also Verbals)
  in, off, over+there, out, with

Pronouns
  (he), (she), (that), (me), (there), (you), (they)[a] . . .

Reflexives
  (herself), (yourself), (himself) . . .

Possessive
  (mine), (hers), (his), (yours)

[a]Signs in parentheses are indexical.

negative which uses the index finger only. During the next 2 months in our videotapes, there was a flowering of different negative signs. Some morphologically related (BAD, DON'T+KNOW, DON'T+WANT) others related by virtue of expressing negation (NOT, NONE, CAN'T, N-O, NOTHING). Of special interest is that during this period, she extracted the common element of the related negative signs, and used this to negate some sentences. We have given this the English gloss of N'T since it seems to be the common component of a number of negative signs, but is not considered a sign in itself (Table 4).

There is another instance of overgeneralization which we have found to be of interest. Again this derives from a particular syntactic property of American Sign Language. We described a large class of verbal signs which can change direction to incorporate subject and/or object – for example, I+LOOK+AT+YOU executed as a single sign. The sign for YOU+LOOK+AT+ME is the same except that the direction of the sign has changed. This is not true of all verbal signs, which have outward motion. Some (like LEAD, FOLLOW, FINGERSPELL) do not change direction when the subject and object are changed. One young deaf child was taught the alphabet by her parents. Her mother would ask her to imitate by signing FINGERSPELL ABC. One time the child protested at first and wanted to finish her cake. Then when she was ready she signed FINGERSPELL turning her hand so it was a directional sign YOU+FINGERSPELL+TO+ME. It is plausible that this is like the overgeneralizations we find in speaking children who use the regular rule for forming past tense (ed) to create forms like *bringed* and *digged*. The child may have discovered the general possibility in sign

TABLE 4
Development of Negation in Signed Sequences

Pola, 2.7–3.0 Years

Ages 2.7 and 2.8 (VT I and II)
Eat no. Old, no. Neg work. Talk, neg. No touch. Touch, no.

Signs used: No and neg

Ages 2.9 and 2.10 (VT III and IV)
Neg right (that). Neg draw know. Neg give+(him), no. Daddy fish, neg. (Me) neg boy, (me) girl. Pola (there) neg, Mother. Neg, (me) eat finish.

Signs used: No and neg, as above.

Ages 2.11 and 3.0 (VT V and VI)
(That) bird, + not duck.   Not broke (that).   (That) not doll, neg.   Not fish, duck. (That) bend Darlene, not Ursula.   (Me) don't + want.   Water, not (me), Rick bring. (Me) none milk.   Ursula where?   None, Ursula.   N't (that) (him). N't (that) Mother name (there).

Signs used: No and *neg* as above. *Not, Don't+want, None, Don't+know, Can't, Bad, N-o, Nothing,* and overgeneralized *n't* (turning hand palm down and moving downward).

language for incorporating subject—object relations into verbal notions, and may have extended this to cases where the adult signer would not. Thus we see that some of the basic processes of language acquisition are the same across modalities.

References

Bellugi, U. Studies in sign language. *American Annals of the Deaf,* (in press).

Bellugi, U. and Klima, E. S. Roots of language in the sign talk of the deaf. *Psychology Today,* June, 1972, 61–64, 76.

Bellugi, U. and Siple, P. Remembering with and without words. In *Current Problems in Psycholinguistics,* Centre National de la Recherche Scientifique, Paris, France, (in press).

Braine, M. D. S. The ontogeny of English phrase structure: The first phase. *Language,* 1963, **39,** 1–13.

Brown, R., Cazden, C., and Bellugi, U. The child's grammar I to III, *Minnesota Symposia on Child Psychology,* Vol. 2, Minneapolis: Univ. of Minnesota Press, 1969.

Brown, R., *Psycholinguistics: Selected papers,* New York: Free Press, 1970.

Chomsky, N. *Syntactic structures.* The Hague, Netherlands: Mouton, 1957.

Gardner, A. R., & Gardner, B. T. Teaching sign language to a chimpanzee. *Science,* 1969, **165,** 664–672.

Hayes, C. *The ape in our house.* New York: Harper, 1951.

Hayes, K. J., & Hayes, C. *Proceedings of the American Philosophical Society,* 1951, **95,** 105–125.

Kellogg, W. N. Communication and language in the home-raised chimpanzee. *Science,* 1968, **162,** 423–427.

Kellogg, W. N., & Kellogg, L. A. *The ape and the child.* New York: McGraw-Hill, 1922.

Lieberman, P. H. Primate vocalizations and human linguistic ability. *Journal of the Acoustical Society of America,* 1968 44, 1574–1584.

Premack, D. The education of S*A*R*A*H. *Psychology Today,* Sept., 1970, 4, 54–58.

Premack, D. Language of chimpanzee? *Science,* 1971, **172,** 808–822.

Slobin, D. I. *Psycholinguistics.* Glenview, Illinois: Scott, Foresman, 1971.

Stokoe, W. C. Sign language structure: An outline of the visual communication systems of the American deaf. *Studies in Linguistics,* Occasional Papers No. 8. Buffalo, New York: Univ. of Buffalo Press, 1960.

Stokoe, W. C., Casterline, D., & Croneberg, C. G. *A dictionary of American sign language on linguistic principles.* Washington, D.C.: Gallaudet Press, 1965.

AFFECTIVE ASPECTS
OF AESTHETIC COMMUNICATION[1]

D. E. Berlyne

Department of Psychology
University of Toronto
Toronto, Canada

Experimental aesthetics, the application of experimental psychology to the arts and other aesthetic phenomena, is now a little over 100 years old (Berlyne, 1972). Deductive or speculative approaches to psychological aesthetics have, of course, been pursued for much longer than that. Nevertheless, psychological aesthetics, whether of the scientific or philosophical variety, has so far accomplished disappointingly little. Past work has supplied a number of ideas and findings that those who are interested in this area of inquiry cannot afford to ignore. But, to all intents and purposes, the area must be confronted as a tract of uncharted virgin territory, for which previous explorers have left only the sketchiest of maps and trailmarkers.

There are many reasons for this lack of progress (see Berlyne, 1971a, Chap. 3). But the heart of the matter seems to be the particularly acute way in which psychological aesthetics presents the two main difficulties faced by students who are studying psychology for the first time. First, they discover themselves to be saddled with presuppositions that must be examined and called in question before they can make progress. These are implicit in the very language used to talk about psychological phenomena, and, more likely than not, they are vestiges of technical psychological theories of bygone eras. Second, students find themselves obliged to work their way through interminable methodological thickets. They come to psychology hoping to receive answers to questions, but, for much of the time, their courses discuss what questions ought to be asked and how the answers should be sought.

[1] The preparation of this chapter and research discussed in it were supported by research grants APA-73 from the National Research Council of Canada and S69-1073 from the Canada Council.

To turn to psychological aesthetics, certain firmly rooted beliefs about the nature and functions of art are so widely taken for granted that they are rarely seen for what they are, i.e., as particular theoretical positions on issues that are open to alternative views. Both technical and popular discussions of art, from the columns of newspaper critics to art-appreciation courses, are riddled with tacit, and therefore insidious, assumptions about the psychology of aesthetic enjoyment.

For one thing, it is customary to insist that aesthetic activities are entirely unlike anything else in life, in fact to treat them as supernatural phenomena that it is sacrilegious to mention in the same breath with other forms of behavior. In all the world's major and minor cultures, the arts have more often than not been ancillary to magic and religion and to the politicophilosophical ideologies that have partly grown out of magic and religion and partly superseded them. And when the independence of art has been proclaimed, as in the "art for art's sake" movement of the 19th century, it has been looked upon with a superstitious awe that turns it into a quasi-religion on its own.

Exponents of psychological aesthetics, apart from some influenced by psychoanalysis or Gestalt theory, have usually dealt with its subject matter in isolation. Their primary interests have almost always been concentrated on other areas of psychology, and they have dabbled in experimental aesthetics as a sideline. There has been little integration of their contributions to aesthetics with the rest of their work.

It is as if we had two different nervous systems, one of which we put on before entering the shrines of art, the other being reserved for more mundane occupations. It is at least as if the nervous system were governed by completely different principles when processing artistic material and when processing anything else. There are, it is true, striking differences between responses to stimulus patterns that are identifiable as "art" and highly similar stimulus patterns that are embedded in "real life," so that some writers have spoken of the peculiarities of the "aesthetic attitude." Nevertheless, the same nervous system is used for both aesthetic and other activities, so that we must surely expect some common principles to govern its functioning in both capacities. If there seems to be a mysterious gap between aesthetic behavior and other behavior, this points to deficiencies in our understanding of how the nervous system works in nonaesthetic contexts. So the psychology of aesthetics must have much to tell us about psychology in general. And other areas of psychology must have much to tell us about aesthetics.

When an area of inquiry has been stagnating or progressing at a snail's pace – and we must acknowledge that psychological aesthetics is such an area – developments outside its boundaries are usually responsible for eventually speeding things up. And, fortunately, several new developments in other fields of psychology, particularly motivation theory, as well as in neurophysiology, anthropology, sociology, and philosophy, are beginning to offer hope that psychological aesthetics may at last be approaching what economists call the "take-off" (Rostow, 1960). In fact the most promising new findings and hypotheses have come from authors who never had the slightest thought of contributing to aesthetics.

It is quite commonly taken as an axiom that creative artists have exceptionally deep or exceptionally insightful emotional experiences or "feelings" and that the prime function of their works is to communicate these as completely as possible to their audience, to induce in others affective reactions that will resemble their own as closely as possible. This aesthetic theory, with its attendant "cult of personality," its implication that art should enable one to share the unique mental processes of an extraordinary human being, has a rather involved history. It can be traced back, through the aesthetic writings of such authors as Ogden and Richards (1923) and Tolstoi (1897–1898), to the Romantics of the early 19th century, with a few earlier precursors such as the Neo-Platonists. Regardless of how valid or invalid this belief is, the point is that other views are possible and that this view would, in fact, have seemed rather strange at other periods of history and in other parts of the world.

Art has often been regarded not as a means to affective communication, but rather as a means of creating pleasing forms or as a means to knowledge about the appearance of external objects or about life in general. It is true that the power of the arts to instill emotion has been recognized since Plato in the west and for a comparable length of time in the major oriental cultures. But at most times and places, it has been assumed that the appropriate use for the emotion-provoking potentialities of art is to inculcate officially approved feelings with respect to religious, political, or ethical matters, rather than the idiosyncratic feelings of artists.

There certainly is a great deal of communication through art. An artist can communicate messages about virtually anything through his work, whether on his own behalf or in the name of his society or subculture. It is widely believed, although we could do with more empirical research on this point, that a message will be communicated more effectively if it is couched in an artistic form. But art may communicate nothing more than the artist's views on what is worth looking at, listening to, thinking about, feeling about, or, in a word, paying attention to.

As for methodology, psychological aesthetics has so far resorted predominantly to two kinds of investigation. Nonexperimental writers have relied on the case-history method. They have looked to detailed examination of specific works of art and of specific artists for confirmation of their theoretical assertions. But anybody with even elementary scientific training is invariably left wondering how representative the sample of cited instances can be and how many instances could have been cited that fail to fit the author's views so well.

There is also the obvious danger that the proud originator of a hypothesis will overlook alternative interpretations or explanations that might be compatible with the facts.

Experimental aestheticians, on the other hand, have for the most part used variants of Fechner's (1876) method of choice. Recently, they have adopted some of the sophisticated procedures for collecting and analyzing data that have come out of modern scaling theory. But whether they use these or the cruder methods of rating, ranking, and comparison that preceded them, it all boils down to asking subjects to indicate verbally how much they "like" a particular stimulus pattern or "prefer" one to another. This kind of work has yielded an impressive body of interesting findings. For one thing, talking or writing about a work of art, whether in laudatory or in pejorative terms, is one of the most conspicuous forms of behavior occasioned by exposure to art. And this kind of evaluative behavior is evidently of great interest to many people, especially to those who depend on the arts for their livelihood. Psychologists, however, have been interested in these verbal judgments mainly because they assumed them, understandably enough, to reflect important motivational or affective processes within the subject, processes that could be expected to govern nonverbal behavior in other situations. But, however reasonable it may be to suppose that verbal evaluative judgments have a great deal to tell us about other reactions to artistic stimulus patterns, we are far from knowing exactly what they have to tell us or which judgments will tell us the most. In other words, there is a need to supplement the study of verbal aesthetic judgments with the study of other, nonverbal responses to aesthetic material. Only in this way can we assess the significance of the information that can be accumulated with such ease and in such abundance through verbal judgments.

How recent advances in motivation theory and in disciplines bordering on psychology can illuminate the psychological and biological roots of the arts has been considered at length elsewhere (Berlyne, 1971a, 1972). All I can do here is to review briefly some recent experiments conducted in our laboratory at the University of Toronto. The findings of these experiments may, I hope, be of some interest, but I am bringing them up now chiefly in view of the methodological problems that they illustrate.

For a number of years, we, and a growing number of investigators in other laboratories, have been examining motivational effects of the so-called "collative" stimulus properties. This term denotes properties like novelty, surprise, complexity, and ambiguity that depend on comparison or collation of several stimulus elements or items of information. Psychologists first had their attention drawn to these variables by experimental work on exploratory behavior in animal and human subjects, since they were soon seen to play a prominent, but by no means exclusive, role in determining the strength and direction of exploratory or stimulus-seeking responses. However, the range and extent of their motivational influence soon became apparent in other areas of research, including personality study, child development, ethology, humor, and play (see Berlyne, 1960, 1963, 1966, 1969).

The collative stimulus properties are readily recognized as the constituents of aesthetic form or structure. "Art" is a concept that has perennially defied attempts at definition, and the label certainly covers a dazzling heterogeneity of objects serving vastly different purposes at different times (Berlyne, 1971a). But when people have attempted to ask what all the phenomena that have been classed as "art" might have in common, they have sooner or later focused on the central motivational role of "structural" or "formal" factors, which means collative variables.

Consequently, although experiments of this kind were not initially prompted by problems relating to art, these experiments can now be recognized as contributions to experimental aesthetics, among other things. They belong to the tradition of what Fechner (1876), the founder of experimental aesthetics, called "aesthetics from below." By this, he meant an approach that begins with the simplest kinds of material and works its way up gradually toward the complexities found in genuine works of art. He contrasted it with the "aesthetics from above" that had been, and still is, characteristic of philosophical aesthetics and art criticism.

Experiments representative of aesthetics from below inevitably stir up problems and criticisms that are, in fact, inseparable from experimental psychology in general. They expose subjects to simple stimuli — visual forms, patches of color, isolated sounds, or brief sequences of sounds — that seem ludicrously artificial and remote from anything that anybody would dream of calling "art." They certainly resemble elements that might be found in works of art, but, taken in isolation, they are abstracted from the networks of relations that would seem to constitute the quintessence of aesthetic structure. However, one cannot have it both ways. The only alternative to aesthetics from below is to examine reactions to genuine works of art — reproductions of paintings, pictures of statues, musical and literary passages. This alternative approach is equally indispensable and must be pursued in parallel. But it also has its serious limitations. Any two paintings, for example, must differ from each other in at least 1001 respects. And if some reliable difference is found between reactions to them, it is difficult to tell which of the 1001 variables or which of the $(2^{1001} - 1)$ combinations of them might be responsible for the effect.

In recent years, one of our primary objectives has been to study the effects of the collative stimulus properties on the various kinds of measures that seem indicative of affective or hedonic response to stimulus patterns and, therefore, of at least one facet of aesthetic appreciation. Such measures fall into three main groups. First, there are verbal judgments, that old standby of experimental aesthetics that we could hardly dispense with even though we have noted their insufficiencies. We have been eliciting judgments of the collative variables themselves to ascertain how the subjective dimensions of novelty, complexity, etc. are related to objective physico-chemical, spatio-temporal, and statistical attributes of stimulus patterns. We have also solicited ratings of pleasingness and of interestingness on 7-point Osgood-type scales. We have concentrated on these two evaluative dimensions, also using others occasionally, because they have regularly provided worthwhile and mutually complementary information.

Second, there are psychophysiological measures, which are recognized as indices of the magnitude of the orientation reaction or of the extent to which arousal is momentarily raised by a stimulus. We have used galvanic skin response (GSR) and duration of electroencephalographic (EEG) desynchronization, and we are embarking on spectrographic analysis of EEG waves.

Third, we have nonverbal somatic measures. These include measures of exploratory behavior, which are clearly relevant to aesthetics. They comprise duration of spontaneous exploration (i.e., looking time or listening time) and exploratory choice (i.e., choice for further inspection among stimulus patterns that have already been exposed). We are also developing techniques for examining the reward value of visual and auditory stimulus patterns, as shown by their ability to reinforce arbitrarily chosen instrumental responses.

Experiments with Visual Patterns

Over the last 10 years or so, research of this nature with visual patterns has been going on not only in our laboratory but in a growing number of laboratories in several different countries (see Berlyne, 1971a, Chap. 13). It is impossible to sum up briefly all the data that have accrued from it. But one or two salient and recurrent findings may be mentioned briefly.

Subjective or judged novelty behaves, on the whole, as one would expect it to behave (Berlyne & Parham, 1968). For example, it declines as a visual pattern appears repeatedly. It revives when a repeated pattern is replaced by one that is a little different, the revival being more marked the greater the contrast. Many psychophysiological studies have likewise shown various indices of the orientation reaction to weaken as a stimulus pattern becomes more familiar and to be restored when it is replaced by something new. Both pleasingness and interestingness seem to follow subjective novelty fairly closely, as far as simple patterns are concerned. But pleasingness rises and then declines as a complex pattern becomes more and more familiar (Berlyne, 1970).

With regard to complexity, which has received much more study than novelty, things are not quite so straightforward (Berlyne, 1971a, Chap. 13). Complexity ratings vary directly with the number of independently selected elements and inversely with the degree of similarity or, more generally, mutual interdependence among elements. Experiments showing more complex patterns to evoke more intense orientation reactions or arousal increments have been accumulating. When subjects are allowed to look at each of a succession of visual patterns for as long as they wish, looking time appears to rise steadily as complexity rises, although there are occasional hints of a leveling off or even a decline as the upper extreme of complexity is approached. Judged interestingness behaves very much like looking time. Judged pleasingness is also strongly affected by complexity, but curves for pleasingness and synonomous attributes (e.g., liking, preference, pleasantness) are strikingly different from interestingness curves. Many investigations have produced an inverted U-shaped curve with maximum pleasingness, etc., coinciding with some moderate degree of complexity. Sometimes, several peaks appear (Munsinger & Kessen, 1964), and there has sometimes been an upward turn in pleasingness near the lower extreme of complexity.

In view of all the weight that has been placed on judgments of pleasingness and the like throughout the history of experimental aesthetics, it is rather ironic that their behavioral correlates remain something of a mystery. Contrary to what some might expect, looking time is closely related to interestingness but not to pleasingness. Some patterns are relatively high in both pleasingness and interestingness, and some are quite pleasing but uninteresting. These are generally simple, geometrical patterns, reminiscent of those that the Gestalt school called "good" or *prägnant* configurations. When subjects have to choose for further viewing one of two patterns to which they have just been exposed, they often choose the more complex item, when it is the more interesting but the less pleasing one (Berlyne, 1963; Berlyne & Crozier, 1971; Berlyne, 1971b). There seem to be some conditions in which the opposite holds, but the situation is far from clear. Certainly, more complex material is likely to be sought out, in preference to simpler and more pleasing material, when curiosity or boredom are at work.

A factor-analytic experiment by Evans and Day (1971) corroborates this general picture. Examining a variety of verbal and nonverbal responses to random polygons with differing numbers of sides, they brought to light a factor with high loadings for objective complexity (i.e., number of sides), subjective (i.e., rated) complexity, GSR, looking time, and judged interestingness. Other verbal ratings showed this factor to be close to Osgood's *activity* dimension. It is presumably also fairly safe to equate it with arousal value, i.e., the power of a stimulus pattern to evoke an arousal increment or orientation reaction. The second factor was evidently close to Osgood's *evaluative* dimension. It covered good–bad, ugly–beautiful, pleasing–displeasing, and likable–dislikable ratings, but none of the nonverbal measures.

Of late, we have sought to establish a link between this experimental literature on visual complexity and a long-standing theme in aesthetic theory: the view that art exploits the special appeal of "uniformity in variety" (Berlyne & Boudewijns, 1971). We used patterns consisting of two colored shapes, appearing either side by side or one after the other. The two elements could resemble each other in from 0 to 4 properties, differing from each other in from 4 to 0. Different subjects rated the patterns on simple–complex, displeasing–pleasing, and uninteresting–interesting scales. The patterns were judged to be more complex the greater number of properties distinguishing their two elements and more complex when presented successively than when presented simultaneously (see Fig. 1). And in accordance with so many other experiments on hedonic effects of visual complexity, rated interestingness turned out to increase more or less monotonically with complexity, while pleasingness was highest at intermediate levels of complexity, i.e., when the two elements possessed both similarities and differences or, in other words, "uniformity in vareity" (see Fig. 2).

Experiments with Single Sounds

There has been much less work on exploratory behavior and related phenomena using auditory stimuli. But we have recently been extending our research to sounds. The most interesting questions concern effects of sound sequences, since this is where factors that play a major role in music, and in aesthetics generally, can be expected to arise. But it seemed necessary to

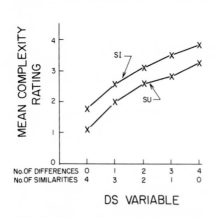

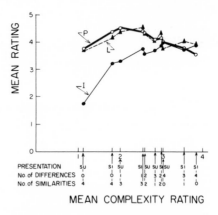

Fig. 1. Mean ratings on simple–complex scale for two-element visual patterns. SU: Successive; SI: simultaneous. (Experiments on uniformity in variety, Berlyne & Boudewijns, 1971.)

Fig. 2. Mean ratings on displeasing–pleasing, dislike–like, and uninteresting–interesting scales for two-element visual patterns. P: Pleasingness; I: interestingness; L: liking; SI: simultaneous; SU: successive. (Experiments on uniformity in variety, Berlyne & Boudewijns, 1971.)

investigate effects of single sounds, varying in pitch and in complexity, as a preliminary task. Some earlier experiments (Berlyne, McDonnell, Nicki, & Parham, 1967) pointed to a U-shaped function relating duration of EEG synchronization to the pitch of sounds equated for loudness. Similar U-shaped curves have been reported by Misbach (1932) and by Schönpflug (1967) using the GSR. Ratings of complexity, pleasingness, and interestingness were also recorded, and several significant effects were detected, but a clear overall picture did not emerge.

A more thorough and systematic study of exploration and verbal rating of single sounds has since been carried out by Lindon Parham, now at Nipissing College, as part of a doctoral project. He gathered a collection of 20 sounds, which were carefully equated for loudness. They included sine-wave tones of several frequencies, consonant and dissonant pairs of sine-wave and square-wave tones, a chord of four sine-wave tones, and white noise.

Two measures of exploratory behavior were derived from different groups of subjects: listening time (the subject heard each sound for as long as he wished before pressing a button to replace it with the next sound) and exploratory choice (the subject heard two sounds, one after the other, for 3 sec. and then pressed a button to bring back one of the sounds). Other groups of subjects were required to rate the sounds for complexity, pleasingness, and interestingness, respectively. Not surprisingly, judged complexity increased with the number of constituent frequencies (being higher for chords of the single sounds) and varied inversely with the extent to which one frequency predominated (being higher for square waves than for sine waves and higher still for white noise). There turned out to be two distinct clusters of significantly intercorrelated dependent variables. One consisted of complexity and interestingness (although white noise was rather anomalous, being rated more complex, but less interesting, than the other sounds). The other consisted of pleasingness, listening time, and exploratory choice.

The close association between listening time and pleasingness and the lack of any firm connection between these two measures and complexity or interestingness contrast remarkably with recurrent findings from experiments with visual patterns. As far as these sounds are concerned, pleasingness seesm to depend mainly on pitch (being greater for lower tones) and on consonance.

Why there should be these sharp differences between effects of visual and auditory complexity is a question that clearly calls for some thought. The answer could have something to do with obvious differences between the ways in which sights and sounds are perceptually processed. We perceive the components of a simultaneous visual pattern separately and proceed to relate them to one another and to organize them into subwholes. The constituents of a simultaneous sound combination, on the other hand, tend strongly to blend into a unity. It is difficult to detect them separately, and we generally have no reason to do so, except perhaps when listening to a musical work for several instruments or voices or when confronted with several people talking at once. Furthermore, in attempting to make sense of a visual pattern, we resort to associative meaning, classifying it in terms of its resemblances with familiar objects. Little of this seems likely to occur with the kinds of auditory stimuli used by Parham, which were not readily identifiable as speech, music, or sounds characteristic of familiar objects.

Experiments with Sound Sequences

The speculations just outlined can be tested by studying responses to sound sequences, which can possess structural properties analogous to those of visual patterns and can offer scope for comparing and grouping of elements. One of our graduate students, John B. Crozier, has recently completed some experiments of this sort. He adopted Parham's dependent variables — namely listening time, exploratory choice, and ratings of complexity, pleasingness, and interestingness. He also obtained ratings on an ugly--beautiful scale. He used two groups of subjects, one consisting of students from the Faculty of Music and the other of students from the Faculty of Arts and Science who were shown by a test to be relatively untutored with respect to music theory.

With respect to the stimulus material, a great deal of time and labor was saved thanks to the cooperation of Dr. Paul C. Vitz of New York University. He had prepared a series of sound sequences, whose component tones varied in frequency, duration, and loudness (Vitz, 1966). By manipulating statistical distributions of different classes of elements, he contrived six levels of "stimulus variation," differing both in uncertainty and in variance with respect to the three properties. When subjects were asked to rate the sequences for "variation or unexpected change," the results concurred with these objective statistical parameters. Other subjects rated the sequences for "pleasantness" on a 9-point scale, and the mean ratings lay on an inverted U-shaped curve. Intermediate levels of stimulus variation were deemed most pleasant, and the peak for subjects of who were trained and interested in music corresponded to a higher variation level than the peak for unmusical subjects.

Crozier verified, first, that rated complexity increases with a significant linear trend over the six levels of what Vitz had called "variation" (see Fig. 3). Furthermore, rated complexity was very close indeed to statistical measures of uncertainty, in bits. The correlation between these two measures — one subjective and the other objective — was +.995 over the six pairs of sequences. Rated interestingness increased with uncertainty (and therefore with rated complexity), following a curve that did not deviate significantly from a straight line (Fig. 4). The curves for the two groups of subjects both approximated

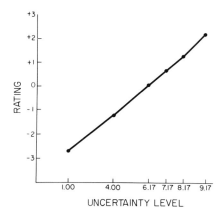

Fig. 3. Mean ratings on simple—complex scale for sound sequences. (Experiments by J. B. Crozier.)

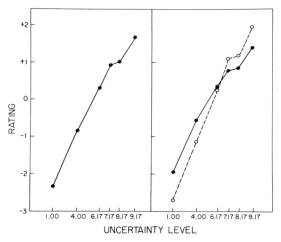

Fig. 4. Mean ratings on uninteresting–interesting scale for sound sequences. Right-hand panel: (●) psychology students; (○) music students. (Experiments by J. B. Crozier.)

straight lines, but the rise was steeper for the music students, presumably reflecting sharper discrimination. The ratings for pleasingness and for beauty, like the ratings for pleasantness that Vitz had collected, produced nonmonotonic curves (Figs. 5 and 6) with significant linear and quadratic trend components. Moreover, as in Vitz's experiment, the curves for the musically sophisticated subjects differed significantly from the curves for the other subjects, reaching peaks at higher complexity levels.

Turning to the nonverbal measures, we find (Fig. 7) that listening time produces a rising curve with the peak at the fourth level of uncertainty and a slight decline over fifth and sixth levels. The curve somewhat resembles the

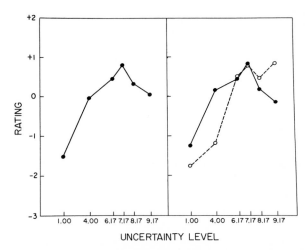

Fig. 5. Mean ratings on displeasing–pleasing scale for sound sequences. Right-hand panel: (●) psychology students; (○) music students. (Experiments by J. B. Crozier.)

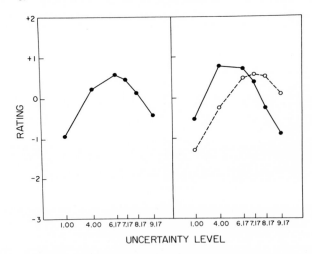

Fig. 6. Mean ratings on ugly–beautiful scale for sound sequence. Right-hand panel: (●) psychology students; (○) music students. (Experiments by J. B. Crozier.)

pleasingness curve (Fig. 5), but the overall rise is more prominent, suggesting a closer connection with interestingness. Partial-correlational and multiple-correlational analysis confirm this impression. Pleasingness and interestingness together account for 80% of the variance in listening time, but of this portion, interestingness accounts for 86% and pleasingness for 14%. The partial correlation of listening time with interestingness (+.81) is significant at the .01 level, but the partial correlation of listening time and pleasingness (+.30) is not

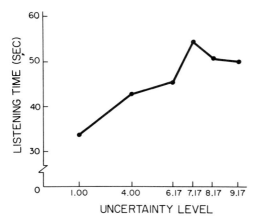

Fig. 7. Mean listening time for sound sequences. Psychology students. (Experiments by J. B. Crozier.)

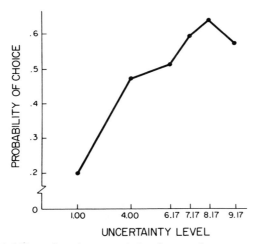

Fig. 8. Probability of exploratory choice for sound sequences. Psychology students. (Experiments by J. B. Crozier.)

significant. In the exploratory-choice procedure, subjects went through 30 trials, on each of which they heard the first 10 sec. of each of two sequences of different complexity levels in turn. They then had to press either of two buttons, thereby choosing to hear one of the sequences continued and completed. Each uncertainty level was paired equally often with every other level, and probability of choice reached a maximum at level 5 (Fig. 8). Once again, the linear and the quadratic components of the trend were significant. Since the data are derived from binary choices, the usual forms of correlational analysis are not applicable, but, once again, the relation seems closer with interestingness than with pleasingness.[2]

Interestingness, Pleasingness, and Exploration

Thus, responses to sequences of sounds show the same strong relation between exploration, on the one hand, and interestingness and complexity, on the other, that has been reported repeatedly by experimenters working with visual patterns. These relations were not apparent in the data collected by Parham with single tones and simultaneous combinations of sounds. We therefore have some support for what previous work on reactions to complexity has intimated, namely that the judged interestingness of a pattern largely reflects the scope it offers for perceptual processing in the form of organizing, assimilating, interrelating, and interpreting it. In short, a pattern seems to be interesting to the extent that it offers initial uncertainty, conflict, or disorientation with some prospect of subsequent relief through perceptual and intellectual effort. A pattern that is altogether clear at first glance (because it is simple, familiar, or expected) is uninteresting. So is one that is so chaotic and bewildering that it offers little hope of yielding to what Bartlett (1932) called "effort after meaning."

It is perhaps worth pointing out how remarkable this state of affairs is. The word "interesting" can be traced back to the Latin verb *interest*, meaning "is of importance." For a long time, the English word "interest" and its derivatives had senses denoting concern or importance, i.e., senses closer to our present-day notion of "selfish" or "vested interest." In the *Oxford English Dictionary*, the earliest reported use of the word "interesting" in its modern sense of "having the qualities which arouse curiosity, engage attention, or appeal to the emotions" is a reference to an "interesting face" in Sterne's *Sentimental Journey* (1768). In French, the modern usage of the verb *"intéresser"* appeared a century earlier.

---

[2] If the midpoint of the simple-complex scale is regarded as a zero point (neither simple nor complex) and a straight line is fitted to the data in Fig. 1, the zero point corresponds to 5.84 bits. This corresponds to an informational flux of 11.68 bits/sec. Maxima occurred for the ugly-beautiful scale at uncertainty level 3 (12.32 bits/sec.), for the displeasing–pleasing scale and for listening time at level 4 (14.32 bits/sec.) and for exploratory choice at level 5 (16.32 bits/sec.). These values may to some extent reflect adaptation-levels depending on the range of uncertainty values used. But it is interesting to compare them with 16 bits/sec., which, it is argued by the German school of informational aesthetics (Frank, 1959), represents the limit of the information-processing capacity of the human nervous system and the prerequisite for maximal aesthetic appeal.

Duncan New Multiple-Range tests confirm that the functions linking scores on the displeasing–pleasing and ugly–beautiful scales, respectively, with uncertainty are non-monotonic. They do not show this for the listening-time function.

Littré's *Dictionnaire de la Langue Française* mentions an instance in Boileau's *Art Poétique* (1664).

To sum up, the concept of interestingness as we now know it is relatively recent. Nevertheless, the way the term is used bears close relation to objective complexity, defined in terms of statistical parameters, to subjective or judged complexity, and to the duration of exploration. On the other hand, words like "please," "like," and "beautiful" have been current in their present senses for many more centuries. Psychologists have devoted much study to verbal ratings using these words, which, it seems, largely measure a common underlying variable. But the behavioral correlates of this variable remain something of a mystery, and much more research is needed to unravel them.

Experiments on Affective Responses to Poetry

Let me now turn to a rather different line of research that may open up broad new prospects for experimental aesthetics. It is often held that works of literature or of representational art serve to change our attitudes to the world in general or to those portions of the external world that they depict. They are said to make us "see" or "feel about" particular objects in new ways, or to give these objects a new "meaning" for us.

One way of testing this kind of assumption was originated by Drake (1970), then an undergraduate at the University of Glasgow. He thought of using Osgood's semantic-differential scales to measure affective reactions to poetry. This technique permits one to locate stimulus objects along Osgood's *evaluative, activity,* and *potency* dimensions. As we saw earlier, the experiment by Evans and Day confirms the impression that the activity dimension has something to do with arousal value and that the evaluative dimension encompasses judgments of pleasingness.

Drake took three poems by leading British poets of the 19th and 20th centuries. They were specifically chosen for what he called "a concrete unitary effect," by which he meant that "there is only one subject on which the poet concentrates remaining in the background himself" and "the poet presents an easily apprehended picture." The Osgood semantic differential was administered to an experimental group of secondary-school students before and after they listened to each poem twice. They were also exposed to a poem especially written for the experiment that was designed to be inferior to the other three. A control group was engaged in unrelated conversation between the fore-test and after-test. The distances in semantic space between the points derived from the ratings were compared for the experimental and control groups. With each poem, the displacement was significantly greater in the experimental than in the control group, and the effect was significantly smaller for the inferior poem.

However, the inferior poem differed in subject matter from the other three poems. So it is possible that the content, rather than the quality of the writing, made the difference.

Drake's method has been subjected to some modifications in an experiment carried out by one of our undergraduates, Susan Nainudel. We took extracts from three poems, Keats' *Ode to Autumn*, Tennyson's *The Brook*, and D. H. Lawrence's *The Snake*. For each of these extracts, we also composed a prose version in which we tried, so far as possible, to conform to normal, unpoetic vocabulary, word order, and sentence structure. But we kept the content of the poetic and prosaic versions as similar as possible by enumerating all the ideas or elements of meaning in the poem and making sure that each also appeared in the prose passage. When 12 judges were asked to rate each passage on a 7-point scale, their ratings confirmed that the original version was in each case judged significantly more "poetic."

Every subject heard, twice each, one poem and the prose passage corresponding to another poem. All six possible combinations of a verse and a prose passage were presented with each of the two possible orders to equal numbers of subjects. After listening to both passages, he went through 45 Osgood scales, comprising, in a random order, five scales indicative of each of Osgood's three dimensions (having low loadings on the other two dimensions) with reference to the concepts "Autumn," "Brook," and "Snake" (see Table 1). One of these concepts had been the subject of the poem just heard, one of the prose passage, and one of neither. In this way, it was possible to separate the effects of the content of a poem by comparing ratings after hearing the poetic or the prosaic version and after hearing neither. Then, a comparison between the effects of the two versions would reveal the influence of poetic form.

The influence of poetic form on factual recall was also studied. After completing the Osgood test, each subject was asked to recall as much as he could of what was in the two passages he had heard. Half of the subjects received the recall test immediately, while the other half received it after a 24-hr. delay.

TABLE 1
Experiments on Affective Responses to Poetry (Osgood Scales Used)

Evaluative dimension	Potency dimension	Activity dimension
Good—bad	Large—small	Fast—slow
Beautiful—ugly	Strong—weak	Active—passive
Sweet—sour	Heavy—light	Hot—cold
Clean—dirty	Rugged—delicate	Sharp—dull
Kind—cruel	Masculine—feminine	Angular—rounded

TABLE 2
Experiments on Affective Responses to Poetry
Percentage of Elements Recalled

	Immediate	Delayed	
Poetry	11.33	12.33	11.67
Prose	18.33	13.33	15.67
	14.67	12.67	13.67

Factual recall was measured, in accordance with the method introduced by Bartlett (1932), by dividing each passage into units of content and deciding how many figured in the effort at recall regardless of wording. In doubtful cases, a score of .5 was given.

It turned out that recall was significantly better after hearing the prose than hearing the poetry (see Table 2). This might have been because the poetic version contained more unfamiliar words or turns of phrase, which impeded learning. It might also have been because concentration on the aesthetically enjoyable form of the poem deflected attention from the factual content. Further work will be needed to pursue these possibilities.

When analyzing the semantic-differential results, we examined the mean ratings over all the five scales corresponding to each of the three dimensions for each of the three concepts. The mean ratings of each concept on each dimension by subjects hearing the poetic version, the prosaic version, and neither were compared. It will be seen (Tables 3 and 4) that, with each concept, at least one dimension revealed a significant difference between subjects hearing the verse or prose passage and subjects hearing neither, implying an affective response to the content. But in no case was there a significant difference between the two versions, suggesting that the content but not the form was influential.

The mean ratings on the three dimensions define a point in three-dimensional semantic space for each concept. The distance between this point and the point of origin or neutral point (corresponding to the midpoint of each scale) can be regarded as a measure of the intensity of the affective response or, to put it differently, the vividness of the image or perception. As Table 4 shows, the poetic and prose passages seem to have increased the intensity of response to "Autumn," but did not change this variable significantly for the other concepts.

We are commonly told that contact with a work of art should leave us permanently changed, that it should have a lasting effect on how we feel or think about a particular subject-matter, rather than merely setting up a transient mood or state of mind that dissipates after a few minutes or hours. This implies that art should promote emotional learning. As argued elsewhere (Berlyne, 1967,

1969), a test conducted at least a day after the termination of a training experience is needed to demonstrate learning effects. This is partly because of the prevalent conception of "learning" as a relatively lasting change in behavior and partly because a day is usually long enough to allow short-lasting phenomena that might otherwise be mistaken for learning effects to die down.

Accordingly, a second experiment was carried out. The procedure was identical to that of the experiment just discussed except that the recall test was omitted and the Osgood scales were filled in approximately 24 hr. after exposure to the recorded passages. At the end, the subjects were also asked to fill in Osgood-type "displeasing–pleasing" and "uninteresting–interesting" scales with reference to each of the passages that they had heard, orders being counter-balanced.

Analysis of variance was applied to the scores for this second experiment, with the delayed test, and for both experiments together. As would be expected, and as Tables 3 and 4 show, the effects of the passages were less pronounced after the delay. However, none of the interactions between the poetry/prose/neither variable and the immediate–delayed variables turned out to be significant. It will be noted that the only concept to show any evidence of an effect outlasting 24 hr. is "Autumn." Subjects who heard either version showed a significantly intensified response (greater distance from point of origin) in the delayed test. And, in both experiments taken together, the effects of the two "Autumn" passages on intensity and on the evaluative score were significant, with no significant interaction to indicate that these effects were weakened by the delay. To sum up, one of our three pairs of passages has provided evidence that a durable change in affective response – i.e., emotional learning – can result from exposure to the content of a poem.

The pleasingness and interestingness ratings did not differ significantly among the three pairs of passages or between the poetic and prosaic version of any passage. It was a little disconcerting to note that we had failed in our efforts to concoct passages that would be evaluated less favorably than the products of three celebrated poets! But this may have to do with the fact that the ratings were made a day after the passages were heard, so that recall of initial evaluations may have dimmed.

There are a number of obvious ways in which work with this potentially fruitful technique can and must be carried further. First, in our experiment, the poetic form seems to have contributed nothing material to the affective response and it detracted from recall. There must be other conditions in which it contributes something positive. Presumably, different kinds of poetic form have different effects with different audiences, and we may very well have chosen poetic styles that do not have much impact on contemporary Canadian undergraduates.

TABLE 3

Mean Osgood Scores after Immediate and Delayed Tests[a]

		Evaluative			Potency			Activity			Distance from origin (intensity)		
		Po[b]	Pr[c]	N[d]	Po	Pr	N	Po	Pr	N	Po	Pr	N
Autumn	Immediate	2.2	1.9	2.9	3.3	3.7	3.7	3.8	3.8	4.1	2.20	2.52	1.86
	Delayed	2.3	2.4	3.0	3.5	3.9	3.6	3.6	3.9	4.0	2.25	2.39	1.71
Brook	Immediate	1.8	1.9	1.9	4.6	4.5	5.2	3.8	3.2	4.6	2.67	2.55	2.94
	Delayed	1.8	2.2	2.0	5.2	4.4	4.6	3.8	3.6	3.6	2.89	2.47	2.43
Snake	Immediate	4.0	3.7	4.7	3.8	4.0	3.0	4.3	4.8	3.5	1.76	1.97	1.90
	Delayed	3.4	4.4	3.9	3.9	3.5	3.3	3.9	4.1	3.8	1.71	1.91	1.59

[a]Lower scores mean *more* favorable evaluation, *more* potency, *more* activity.   [b]Po: After hearing *poetic* version.
[c]Pr: After hearing *prosaic* version.   [d]N: After hearing *neither* version.

TABLE 4

Experiments on Affective Responses to Poetry Significant F Values for (Po + Pr) versus N contrast[a]

	Evaluative			Potency			Activity			Distance from origin (intensity)		
	Imm.	Delayed	Both	Imm.	Delayed	Both	Imm.	Delayed	Both	Imm.	Delayed	Both
Autumn	6.55**	—	4.94*	—	—	—	—	—	—	4.95*	7.74***	6.66***
Brook	—	—	—	4.44*	—	—	9.33****	—	—	—	—	—
Snake	4.87*	—	—	5.00*	—	—	6.58**	—	—	—	—	—

[a]1 and 36 *df* for immediate; 1 and 36 *df* for delayed; 1 and 90 *df* for both;   *p < .05,   **p < .025,   ***p < .01,   ****p < .005.

Conclusions

As these experiments illustrate — and other work that is going on all over the world could be cited in support of the same conclusion — we now have at our disposal a number of new experimental techniques and new problems that promise accelerated progress in experimental aesthetics from now on. We can, in fact, speak of the "new experimental aesthetics" and, without slighting the pioneering efforts of our predecessors, nurture hopes of coming nearer to the heart of the aesthetic phenomenon than they were able to do.

Today, many people are clamoring for "relevance" in psychology and other behavioral sciences. Their view of relevance is all too often a dangerously short-sighted one. All the ways in which science has affected human life, whether beneficially or detrimentally, can, without exception, be traced back to researches that did not have this aim and would not at the time have been recognized as practically and socially consequential. But although we must resist the fashionable disparagement of basic and specialized research, we must recognize that the current distribution of psychological man-hours among research topics bears little relation to any conceivable criterion of relative importance. Aesthetics is a prime example of an area receiving much less attention than it warrants. We have only to think of the universality of aesthetic activities in all known human societies, present and past, and the enormous economic and human resources that are expended on them. And, to bring up an argument that should carry even more weight, the absence of any obvious biological necessity for aesthetic activities can only mean that the psychology of aesthetics has much to reveal to us about fundamental characteristics of the human organism.

Many people feel profoundly uncomfortable about the application of experimental methods to the study of art. The behavioral sciences seem to them to be debasing the arts, polluting the Kastalian spring, using a sledge-hammer to dissect butterfly wings, at best to be dealing with superficialities. However, although mining engineers have been hard at work since the Bronze Age, they have no way of penetrating to the depths that does not begin with scratching the surface!

Experimental aesthetics stirs up with particular sharpness common dissatisfactions with contemporary psychology in general, as well as with other disciplines that investigate human life empirically. Psychologists are often expected to provide penetrating analyses of emotional experience, wisdom to face life's perplexities, insightful commentaries on the human condition. Writings on the psychology of art, it is commonly assumed, should be particularly rich in these commodities. But the last place where they are to be found is in the works of experimental psychologists, who have no pretensions in these directions. There are, however, many psychologists — some of them trained and qualified, some of them highly professionalized amateurs – who do their best to supply them. They are, of course, competing with the great novelists, dramatists, poets and essayists of the past and the present. They are trying hard, and what they come up with is often interesting. But they do not yet seem to have produced much to threaten the business of the giants of literature and the other arts. The fact of the matter is that the methods of science are needed to answer the important but circumscribed questions that scientific investigation alone can answer, and the talents of the artist are needed for the indispensable, but likewise limited, functions of art. It is very hard to carry out either of these tasks successfully. It is hardly practicable to accomplish both at once.

References

Bartlett, R. C. *Remembering.* London and New York: Cambridge Univ. Press, 1932.

Berlyne, D. E. *Conflict, arousal and curiosity.* New York: McGraw-Hill, 1960.

Berlyne, D. E. Motivational problems raised by exploratory and epistemic behavior. In S. Koch (Ed.), *Psychology – A study of science.* Vol. 5. New York: McGraw-Hill, 1963.

Berlyne, D. E. Curiosity and exploration. *Science,* 1966, **153,** 25–33.

Berlyne, D. E. Arousal and reinforcement. In D. Levine (Ed.), *Nebraska Symposium on Motivation, 1967.* Lincoln, Nebraska: Univ. of Nebraska Press, 1967.

Berlyne, D. E. The reward value of indifferent stimulation. In J. T. Tapp (Ed.), *Reinforcement and behavior.* New York: Academic Press, 1969.

Berlyne, D. E. Novelty, complexity and hedonic value. *Perception & Psychophysics,* 1970, **8,** 279–286.

Berlyne, D. E. *Aesthetics and psychobiology.* New York: Appleton, 1971. (a)

Berlyne, D. E. Effects of auditory pre-choice stimulation on visual exploratory choice. *Psychonomic Science,* 197, **25,** 193–194. (b)

Berlyne, D. E. Experimental aesthetics. In P. C. Dodwell (Ed.), *New Horizons in Psychology* II. Harmondsworth: Penguin, 1972.

Berlyne, D. E., & Boudewijns, W. J. A. Hedonic effects of uniformity in variety. *Canadian Journal of Psychology,* 1971, **25,** 195–206.

Berlyne, D. E., & Crozier, J. B. Effects of complexity and pre-choice stimulation on exploratory choice. *Perception & Psychophysics,* 1971, **10,** 242–246.

Berlyne, D. E., & Parham, L. C. C. Determinants of subjective novelty. *Perception & Psychophysics,* 1968, **3,** 415–423.

Berlyne, D. E., McDonnell, P., Nicki, R. M., & Parham, L. C. C. Effects of auditory pitch and complexity on EEG desynchronization and on verbally expressed judgments. *Canadian Journal of Psychology,* 1967, **21,** 346–367.

Drake, P. F. Affective reactions to poetry. Paper presented at IV International Colloquium of Empirical Aesthetics, Glasgow, 1970.

Evans, D. R., & Day, H. I. The factorial structure of responses to perceptual complexity. *Psychonomic Science,* 1971, **22,** 357–359.

Fechner, G. T. *Vorschule der Ästhetik.* Leipzig: Breitkopf & Härtel, 1876.

Frank, H. *Informationsästhetik.* Quickborn: Schnelle, 1959.

Misbach, L. E. Effect of pitch of tone-stimuli upon body resistance and cardio-vascular phenomena. *Journal of Experimental Psychology,* 1932, **15,** 167–183.

Munsinger, H., & Kessen, W. Uncertainty, structure and preference. *Psychological*

Monographs, 1964, 78, No. 9. (Whole No. 586)

Ogden, C. K., & Richards, I. A. *The meaning of meaning*. New York: Harcourt, 1923.

Rostow, W. *Stages of economic growth*. London and New York: Cambridge Univ. Press, 1960.

Schönpflug, W. Adaptation, Aktiviertheit and Valenz. Unpublished manuscript, Ruhr University, 1967.

Tolstoi, L. N. Chto takoe isskustvo? *Voprosy filosofii i psikhologii*, 1897–1898. [*What is art?* London: Brotherhood Publ., 1898.]

Vitz, P. C. Affect as a function of stimulus variation. *Journal of Experimental Psychology*, 1966, 71, 74–79.

THE COMMUNICATION OF AFFECT
AND THE POSSIBILITY
OF MAN–MACHINE AS A NEW DYAD

Irwin M. Spigel

Department of Psychology
Erindale College
University of Toronto
Toronto, Canada

The communication of affect in the instructional dyad has received relatively scant attention, despite the fact that such a variable is of concern from both social and educational viewpoints. In addition, the wider acceptance of the ubiquitous machine in educational as well as personal and professional life raises more interesting questions in connection with its use by humans. Until now, for example, the punishment of machines by their users has been confined to studies concerned with "displacement" and other broader areas of psychologically adjustive behavior.

While the findings of studies such as those currently proposed are applicable to education in general, the question of immediacy becomes relevant by virtue of the increasing impact of automation in the instructional environment. One need only visit the exhibit halls at any educational meeting or convention to appreciate the magnitude of hardware influence on what is essentially a personal and social interaction. This becomes even more critical in areas of high urban density where such automated techniques seem to make their most immediate and widespread penetration. In short, the greater the demands for expeditiousness made (i.e., large urban areas) upon the educational system, the more likely it is that new techniques aimed at increasing instructional efficiency will be introduced. It thus becomes more important to ascertain the human factors which are themselves variables in the increasing interaction of men and hardware; specifically, in this case, in situations which are likely to confront those charged with educational responsibilities.

The current series of studies really asks two questions. First, does the pattern of feedback from a subject alter in any way a human's use of punishment when he is charged with the responsibility of teaching someone – anyone – something? Second, will the human's use of punishment be modified in any way if he believes he is communicating with a machine rather than another human? In a way, the second question reduces to that of whether under similar situations, a human will tend to deal with a machine in a similar or different manner than with another human being.

Although the literature abounds with references to aggressiveness, hostility and frustration, little is of immediate applicability to the current study. That is not to say they are irrelevant – merely inapplicable in any imminent way. The closest relative to the present experiment appears to the work conducted by Buss (1961, pp. 47–51) using his "aggression machine." In these experiments, using a mild deception, Buss found that the intensity of electric shock that his subjects believed they were administering to others in a learning situation, was an index of aggressiveness; more aggressive subjects administered higher levels of shock. Unlike Buss' experiments, the current study was not intended as an examination of aggressiveness, nor the applicability of this situation to laboratory investigation of aggression. In any case, the realistic value of such studies is questionable owing to the unusual nature of electric shock as a convenient or even acceptable device in social communication.

One study which seems tangentially related to the current work is described in a technical report and research bulletin prepared by Myers, Gibb, and McConville (1963). In their examination of game interactions, some subjects were told that the other player was a machine, and the remainder informed of human competition. Subjects were found to perform far better when their opponent was a "machine." "Human" others induced more irrationality than "machine" opponents. Under a different instructional set, it was also determined that *cooperation* with "humans" was significantly more successful than cooperation with "machines."

In this connection, several other studies deserve note. Gunderson (1968), speaking from a more philosophical point of view, concluded that it may be relevant for machines someday to show sentience as well as sapience for appropriate man–machine interaction. McClelland (1967) has suggested that in order to understand human behavior by way of simulation, models that reflect a greater comprehension of the interactive capacities of man and machine must be developed.

Experiment 1

Method

Neither the subject population nor the deceptive ploy is particularly original in this experiment. Twenty male students taking introductory psychology courses were employed. A week prior to experimental participation, subjects were called together in small groups and told that they were *experimenters* rather than *subjects*. They were also told at this session that in half their cases, they would be paired with other male students who were to remain unidentified and who would be their subjects. For this reason, they were told that they must not discuss the information they were about to receive with classmates, since it was possible this would contaminate their unidentified subject pool. Subjects were also told at this session that those who were not paired with human learners would be paired with a computer which had been "programmed to respond in the manner of a human being." Subjects were told that it was vital that they appear at the appointed time, since it was imperative that the time of neither their matched "subject," elsewhere in the building, nor the "computer," for which the experimenter was paying, be wasted. Subjects were also told that only when they appeared for the experiment would they learn whether another human or the computer would be their learner. Before leaving this briefing session, the students were told to take home and reread the instructions which they had been given, and once more cautioned to maintain secrecy.

Specifically, student subjects were told that they were to teach a human or computer learner a simple logic task, the instructions for which were already printed so that all they had to do was read them over a microphone. Each was told that this microphone would be open only until all the instructions had been read, and that this would be their only voice communication with the learner. However, each student was told that the experimenter's assistant, who was to be seated at a console behind him, would remain in voice contact with the learner throughout the experiment. Moreover, to add credibility to the student-teachers' task, they were told that this system represented a preliminary attempt at developing a pedogological device of the future.

At this point, the actual logic task was explained. The subjects were told that the learner would have two keys (Key 1 and Key 2) and that the latter would have to press one, both, or neither of the keys in conformance with lettered instructions delivered by the former. There were five such lettered instructions.

Letter A, that is if letter A were flashed: Press Key 1 or Key 2.
Letter B, that is if letter B were flashed: Press Key 1 and Key 2.
Letter C, that is if letter C were flashed: Press Key 1 only.
Letter D, that is if letter D were flashed: Press Key 2 only.
Letter E, that is if letter E were flashed: Press no Key at all.

During the task to follow, *pairs* of letters were to be presented by the subjects to their learners with the latter instructed or programmed to press the key or keys which conformed to the greatest restrictions imposed by the lettered instructions. For example, if the letters E and C were presented then Key 1 would be the correct answer, since it meets the greatest restrictions.

Subjects were told they would receive a computer-generated, random list of pairs to present to the learner. They were also told in the cases where the learner was a computer which was programmed to respond "in the manner of a human being," the key-pressing was internally automated. In this briefing session, the apparatus to be used by the subjects was in full view and the manner in which keys were to be depressed and letters flashed to the learners thoroughly explained.

Finally, after this task orientation, each subject received details about the remainder of his experimental obligation. In front of him, at the apparatus console for the delivery of lettered instructions, was a set of eight verbal responses and a box containing eight switches, each switch relating to a particular verbal response:

Number 1: "I'm afraid that was not correct. Please let us try again."

Number 2: "No. That was an incorrect response. Let us continue."

Number 3: "That was incorrect. You must pay more attention to the instructions. Let us go on."

Number 4: "No. Wrong. You must pay more attention to the instructions. It is important for your success that you respond in the manner which most fully conforms to the restrictions. Let us go on."

Number 5: "No. That was wrong. You must pay more serious attention to the instructions. You will not succeed unless you respond in the manner which most closely and fully conforms to the restrictions placed upon your response. I repeat, attend to instructions and restrictions imposed by the letters."

Number 6: "No. Quite wrong. It is obvious that you either do not understand the restrictions contained in the instructions, or are simply not attending to them. Your successful achievement is based entirely upon your appropriate response to the restrictions imposed by the lettered instructions. Your response was inappropriate. I suggest you think carefully before you respond. Now, attend to the instructions as we continue."

Number 7: "Yes, that is correct."

Number 8: "Yes, I think you understand the principle underlying the correct response."

It can be seen that although the last responses were positive responses, the remaining six responses were negative (punitive, if you will), with each response being more punitive than the one preceding it.

Next, it was explained that the apparatus was designed to indicate automatically whether the learner had responded correctly or incorrectly. A correct response was indicated by a green light, an incorrect response by a red light. The subjects were told that this was accomplished by "computerized internal automation."

Subjects were told that they were to deliver any one of the eight verbal responses to their learner after receiving information concerning whether the learner had responded correctly or incorrectly to a letter pair. This delivery of verbal responses was to be accomplished by pressing the switch corresponding to the response selected. The subjects were told that the selected verbal response would then be presented to the human or computer learner on a closed-circuit television screen. In other words, following the response, the experimenter would be informed automatically of whether his "subject" performed correctly or incorrectly and was, consequently, free to deliver any of the verbal responses by way of switch selection.

There were, of course, no real learners at all. The feedback pattern of correct or incorrect responses from the supposed learners was prearranged and delivered by the assistant, who, it may be recalled, was sitting to the rear, out of sight of the subject and maintaining standby voice communication with the learner, should the need for such communication arise, and ostensibly controlling timing of stimulus presentation. To add to the realism, the lists of lettered-instruction pairs handed the subjects were on actual computer-output paper.

There were four groups of subjects in the study, with five subjects randomly assigned to each. Two of the groups were told they were to teach unidentified classmates the logic task, while students in the remaining two groups were told that a computer "programmed to respond in the manner of a human being" was at the other end. There were a total of 25 trials for each subject. In one of the "computer" and one of the "human" groups, the feedback patterns of correct and incorrect responses approximated a learning curve over the first 20 trials. That is, there were four incorrect responses in Trials 1 to 5, two incorrect responses in Trials 6 to 10, three incorrect responses in Trials 11 to 15, and only one incorrect response in Trials 16 to 20. In the remaining "human" and "computer" groups, incorrect responses were distributed in semirandom fashion across the first 20 trials, rather than being concentrated in the early trials as in the learning-curve pattern. In this semirandom sequence, Trials 1 to 5 contained only one incorrect response; Trials 6 to 10, three incorrect responses; Trials 11 to 15, two incorrect responses; and Trials 16 to 20, four incorrect responses. For all subjects in all groups, Trials 21 to 24 were incorrect responses, and the last, Trial 25, was a correct response.

Thus the four groups constituted a $2 \times 2 \times 3$ design; with *"human"versus "computer"* conditions as one dimension; *learning-curve versus semirandom* as another; and repeated measures over blocks of incorrect responses as the third. The data analyzed were the punitive levels; that is, the number rank of the verbal response (1 to 6) returned by subjects to their learners following incorrect responses. In actuality, the choice of punitive response level was recorded by the assistant on his console, the apparatus being wired to communicate this information to him. A mean level of punitiveness was obtained for each subject on blocks of incorrect responses. Blocks consisted of incorrect responses 1–5; 6–10; and for the final grouping, 11–14, since the last response was a correct in all cases. Positive responses (7 and 8) to correctly answered instruction pairs were also recorded.

Results and Discussion of Experiment 1

This was an exploratory experiment; no specific hypothesis was stated, although there was some idea or anticipation of what might be found. It was, of course, expected that highest levels of punitive reactivity would occur in the final block, owing to the concentration of four successive incorrect responses at a point in the sequence where humans or computers would have been expected by the subjects to have learned what the task was all about, and how to respond successfully. This expectation was confirmed.

However, the most striking observation was that it made no difference at all to our subjects whether they were instructing humans or computers. The students offered punitive verbal feedback, regardless of the target of their instruction. In short, humans and machines were reacted to in virtually identical fashion. The second observation consisted in the fact that it did not appear to matter whether the incorrect responses dropped out in the manner of a learning curve or in semirandom fashion. In other words, the pattern of incorrect feedback had virtually no influence on the level of punitive reactivity. In all cases, punitive level began low in the first block, progressed to a higher level in the second, and reached a peak in the final block. This effect was independent of either the source or pattern of the responding target.

Figure 1 shows the data with the sources combined; that is, human and computer subjects averaged over the two feedback sequences. In Fig. 2 the data for combined feedback patterns over both human and computer subjects are presented.

The $2 \times 2 \times 3$ analysis of variance yielded a highly significant F ratio across blocks of incorrect responses only ($F = 40$; $df = 2, 32, p < .001$). Neither of the remaining dimensions nor their interactions accounted for any appreciable variance.

It should also be pointed out at this time that a binomial test of positive response Number 7 against positive response Number 8 was also carried out for correct responses over the first 20 trials; and on the 25th trial, which, it will be recalled, is the only correct response in the final five trials. In both cases the less rewarding response (Number 7) proved to outweigh response Number 8 ($p < .01$). That is, in a highly significant fashion, all subjects chose the less rewarding response when their learners responded correctly to the instructional pairs.

Of course, the point at which differences were expected to appear between groups was in the second block of incorrect responses. If not in the difference between "computer" and "human" subjects, then perhaps differences might have been expected in reactivity to a familiar learning pattern (the learning curve) as against a semirandom distribution of responses, which indicated no

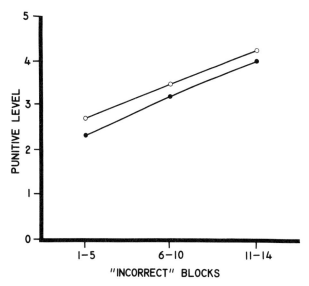

Fig. 1. Mean punitive level for combined "human" and "computer" subjects over the three blocks of "incorrect" trials. (○) Learning curve; (●) random responses.

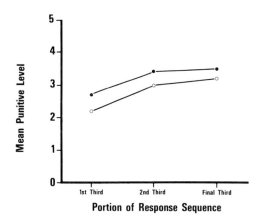

Fig. 2. Mean punitive level for combined response patterns over the three blocks of "incorrect" trials. (●) Human; (○) computer.

systematic demonstration of learning on the part of the learner. The subtle intrusion of personality, ego, and frustration variables was not considered, and it is not really known to what extent subjects' own task—self interactions and dynamics contributed to the observations. However, in questioning subjects afterward, it was ascertained that the deception employed was successful. Several students even commented to the effect that even when told there was a machine at the other end, they felt "as though they were communicating with a human."

Experiment 2

A second experiment was performed to examine the consistency of the preliminary findings and to determine what, if any, effect a greater range of "positive" responses would have on the results. Eight groups of six subjects each were constituted from among first-year male student volunteers. The same general procedure was followed as in the earlier experiment, with half the subjects told they were to instruct another student, and the other half a machine "programmed to respond in the manner of a human." Two other learning-curve-type response feedback patterns and two different random-response patterns were employed. As in the first experiment, the list concluded with four incorrect responses and a correct response.

The six "punitive" messages of the first experiment were retained, but the number of positively reinforcing statements was increased from two to four. The four positive messages follow:

Number 7:   "Yes, That is correct."
Number 8:   "Yes. That is correct. I think you grasped the principle underlying the correct response."
Number 9:   "Good. You were quite correct. Your response was a positive indication of your understanding the task and the underlying principles."
Number 10: "Very good. That response was quite correct. It is becoming much more obvious that you are mastering the task, attending to it carefully, and are efficiently in command of the underlying principles."

Results and Discussion

The resulting mean punitive levels from the first to the second block of incorrect responses showed the same highly significant increase as revealed in the earlier experiment ($F = 18.61$, $df = 2, 80$, $p < .001$). As in the first, there were no differences with respect to "computer" versus "human" (Fig. 3), nor with respect to learning curve as against random responses (Fig. 4). Unlike the first

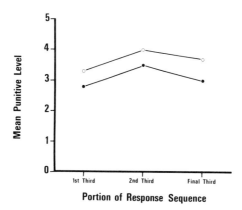

Fig. 3. Mean punitive level for combined response patterns over the three blocks of "incorrect" trials. (●) Human; (○) computer.

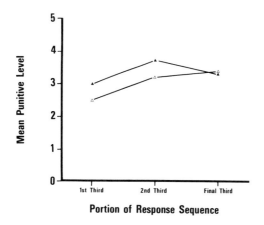

Fig. 4. Mean punitive level for combined "human" and "computer" subjects over the three blocks of "incorrect" trials. (●) Semirandom; (○) learning curve.

experiment, however, there was no significant difference from the second to the third block – i.e., to the last four successive "incorrect" responses presented to all subjects in all groups.

To complicate matters, there was a significant interaction $(F = 2.63,$ $df = 6, 80, p < .05)$ for response patterns by blocks of incorrect responses. Subsequent median tests indicated that the source of significant variation was the continued relatively high punitive level for the "random response" patterns from the second to the third block of incorrect responses, coupled with a reduction in this level for those presented with a "learning-curve" pattern $(X^2 = 5.2, p < .01)$.

Since the fundamental difference between the first and second experiments lay in the wider range of "positive" feedback in the latter, a separate analysis of the subjects' mean "positive" response level was carried out. This yielded a significant difference for patterns, with subjects in the "learning-curve" groups showing – not unexpectedly – higher "positive" feedback levels than those presented with random response patterns $(F = 5.08, df = 3, 40, p < .01)$.

One might conclude that after delivering higher level "positive" messages to their learners, subjects were less inclined to be as punitive as those for whom a consistently higher punitive level was employed prior to the terminal block of incorrect responses. This, of course, requires further study with more varied feedback patterns.

In both experiments, however, there was a dramatic consistency in the increasing punitive level from the first to the second block of incorrect responses, and no difference whatsoever in these levels whether subjects thought a machine or another human was the target of their instruction.

It would appear that subjects, given exposure to whatever techniques have been employed in their own development and socialization in both school and home, still view a punitive attitude as a favoured, even if not especially pedagogically communicative, device. And they use it with increasing vehemence, if not with outright impunity, nor with regard to the demonstrated course or progress of learning.

Acknowledgment

The author wishes to acknowledge the assistance of Gregory Mazuryk and Paul Fairgrieve who aided in the performance of the experiments described.

References

Buss, A. H. *The psychology of aggression.* New York: Wiley, 1961.

Gunderson, K. Robots, consciousness, and programmed behaviour. *British Journal for the Philosophy of Science*, 1968, 19, 109–122.

McClelland, W. A. Training research utilizing man–computer interactions: promise and reality. *Hum R.R.O. Professional Paper*, 1967, No. 23–67.

Myers, A. E., Gibb, C. A., & McConville, C. B. Game interactions with "humans and machines" and their relations to tactical behaviour and success. *Technical Report and Research Bulletin*, O.N.R. Contract No. 2959(00).

DEVELOPMENT OF AFFECT
IN DOGS AND RODENTS[1]

J. P. Scott and V. J. De Ghett[2]

Department of Psychology
Bowling Green State University
Bowling Green, Ohio

Introduction

Social behavior may be defined as behavior stimulating or being stimulated by a member of the same species. Similarly, communication is the transference of information from one individual to another, usually of the same species. In terms of stimulation and response, information may be regarded as a stimulus and the response an indication that the information has been received. Therefore a great deal, if not all, of social behavior can be conceived as communication and analyzed accordingly.

In turn, affect may be defined as feeling, the sensation of an internal state or process. To the extent that such feelings are stimulated by, or are transmitted to, others of the same species, affect may also be considered as social behavior. Obviously not all affect is stimulated by other individuals, an example being the response to the sight of a beautiful sunset. Here, the affect may or may not be communicated to another individual.

More generally, the various kinds of affect may be conceived as internal response systems that function to reinforce certain kinds of experiences either positively or negatively. With respect to its relationship to communication, affect can be considered either as the result of communication or as an internal stimulus that leads to communication. A more direct relationship is involved in

[1] The research reported in this paper was supported in part by Grant HD-3778 from the National Institute of Child Health and Human Development.

[2] Present address: Department of Psychology, State University of New York, Potsdam, New York.

129

the problem of the communication of affect; i.e., the transference of a feeling state from one individual to another.

While affect is one of the major factors modifying human behavior, and by implication one that also plays a major role in the behavior of at least the higher vertebrates, it is one of the least studied by experimental scientists because of the difficulty of objective measurements. These difficulties are magnified in nonhuman animals that cannot report their feelings verbally. A major break-through in this field was the technique of intracranial self-stimulation developed by Olds (1958), through which it is possible for an animal to indicate its responses to sensations induced by electrical stimulation of the brain. Combined with the technique of intracranial stimulation in a free social situation developed by Delgado, it is possible to study the results of affect even in nonverbal animals (Plotnik & Delgado, 1971). The possibilities opened up by these techniques are by no means exhausted.

Still another opportunity for studying affect is afforded by the development of young mammals in both seminaturalistic and experimental conditions. Because of its helplessness, it is usually adaptive for a highly social young mammal to transmit rather than conceal its internal sensations. Consequently there is often a one-to-one correspondence between affect and care-soliciting or et-epimeletic behavior in infants. When hungry, cold, in pain, or alone, the young mammal shows distress vocalization or an equivalent signal which has the function of signalling for help, usually provided by its mother. Lambs bleat, puppies yelp, babies cry, and even young rodents utter supersonic cries.

For some years we have been studying such behavior in the young dog, and in particular the reaction to separation from close social relatives and familiar surroundings. In this chapter we shall discuss some of these findings in relation to communication and compare the results with similar studies in young rodents.

Development of Distress Vocalization in the Dog

Periods of Behavioral Development in the Puppy

Developmental changes in distress vocalization can best be appreciated against the background of the general framework of behavioral development in the dog. A detailed observational study of five pure dog breeds and hybrids between two of them was performed on several hundred puppies from birth to 16 weeks of age (Scott & Fuller, 1965). Changes in sensory, motor, and learning capacities were recorded as well as the appearance of social behavior patterns. On this basis, the early behavioral development of the dog can be divided into three periods. In the *neonatal* period, extending from birth to approximately 2 weeks of age, the young puppy is both blind and deaf, its motor capacities consist chiefly of a slow crawl, and its principal pattern of behavior is that associated with nursing. Despite being deaf, the puppy vocalizes frequently and loudly.

The first changes in behavior are correlated with the opening of the eyes, occurring at an average age of approximately 13 days. Throughout the next 6 or 7 days there is a rapid series of behavioral changes, which characterize this as a *transition* period, in which the adaptive responses of the puppy change from those that are useful in the highly protected environment provided by maternal care to behavior patterns that are adaptive in more independent adult life. By a week after it has first opened its eyes the puppy is not only able to hear, but can walk, wag its tail, and respond to objects at a distance. Behaviorally, it is now recognizable as a young dog. There is also an important change in the capacity to form emotional attachments.

The period of *primary socialization* which follows extends from about 3 to 12 weeks, with a peak capacity for forming rapid attachments occurring between 6 and 8 weeks, just before the time when the emotional response of fear of strange objects begins to appear. This period is marked by the development of two kinds of affective responses, distress vocalization elicited by the absence of the familiar, occurring early in the period, and fear of the strange, which develops strongly in the latter half and has the effect of limiting the capacity to make new social attachments (Scott, 1962). Thus this period becomes a critical one for the determination of primary social relationships. At 12 weeks, the *juvenile* period begins, during which the puppy becomes increasingly independent; the end of this period is marked by sexual maturity.

Vocalization in Response to Discomfort

During the neonatal period, the young puppy vocalizes in a variety of situations, despite the fact that it does not respond to externally produced sounds and is deaf. More specifically, the puppy vocalizes in response to cold, hunger, and pain. Our only systematic study of reactions to discomfort (Scott & Fuller, 1965) was made in connection with weekly weighings of puppies from birth through 4 weeks of age. Each puppy was placed on a metal platform balance for a period of 1 min, and the number of vocalizations counted. Vocalization was apparently a response to contact with the cold metal.

In general, the number of vocalizations declined from week to week, probably influenced in part by the fact that as the puppies grew older they could stand up and had contact with the cold metal only with their feet. Large breed differences were apparent, but these showed no correlation with the vocalization patterns of adults. For example, at 1 week of age, basenjis, which are very nearly barkless as adults, showed the highest rate of vocalization, while beagles, which are very noisy as adults, showed the lowest. These differences probably arise from differences in sensitivity to cold, the basenjis being relatively thin, short-haired dogs, whereas beagles, even as puppies, are relatively fat and hence well insulated from cold.

Separation Distress

During the neonatal period, as long as the puppies are comfortably warm and well fed, they can be isolated in either their home pens or in strange situations and remain completely silent. This sharply contrasts with their behavior in similar situations at 3 weeks of age. Within a minute after being separated from its littermates and placed in either a familiar or unfamiliar situation, a puppy begins to vocalize and continues to do so over long periods. The rate is much higher in unfamiliar physical surroundings.

We have recently done a series of experiments to determine how early this reaction begins (Stewart, DeGhett, & Scott, 1970). The ability to give the separation distress response depends on the ability to discriminate between familiar and unfamiliar situations. Visual discrimination cannot be employed before the eyes open (estimated at 13.0 ± 2.3 days, Scott, 1958), and auditory discrimination depends on the capacity to respond to sound (19.5 ± 2.3 days). In the experiment, puppies are placed in isolation for 10-min. periods under two conditions, being kept comfortably warm ($80-85°F$) in each, since cold itself will elicit vocalization. The first condition is the home nest box, where the puppy can detect the absence of mother and littermates at first through absence of contact, and later through sight and sound. The second condition is a similar nest box in a different room, the box being lined with a clean turkish towel, thus providing differences in both olfactory and tactile cues, to the latter of which puppies can respond discriminantly even the neonatal stage, as shown by Bacon and Stanley (1970).

As in puppies of 21 days or older, response levels in the home pen are consistently lower than in the strange pen and, as one might expect with a lower level of arousal, responses are much more variable and inconsistent. Using comparable criterion levels, changes in the home pen occur at least a day or two later than in the strange pen, where a greater number of cues are available. In general, the ability to give the emotional response appears to be present at least in a weak form, and at least in some animals, as early as 5 days of age. But the development of a strong response is dependent on the development of visual and auditory capacities, since it is during their development that most animals begin to show the response. One of the most interesting findings is that in these early stages average vocalization rates gradually increase from day to day (see Fig. 1), in contrast to the situation at 3 weeks and later, when repeated daily experiences result in a decline of the rate, presumably due to either habituation, familiarization, or a combination of the two (DeGhett, Stewart, & Scott, 1970).

Causes of Separation Distress

The situations that elicit separation distress have been reviewed elsewhere (Scott & Bronson, 1964). Originally Fredericson (1950), who first called

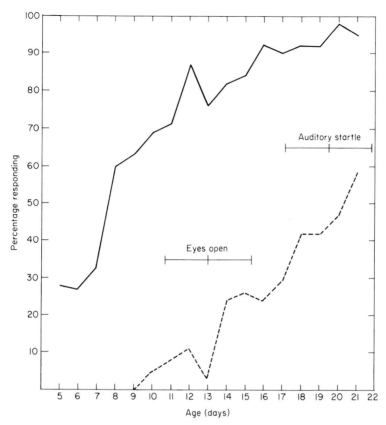

Fig. 1. Percentages of animals responding with different levels of distress vocalization. (−) Animals giving 50 or more responses; (- - -) 800 or more responses per 10-min. period; both in strange room.

attention to this phenomenon, thought it was due to confinement and restriction of movement, since he had placed his separated puppies in small cages. However, a series of experiments on cage sizes indicated no relationship between the degree of restriction and the amount of vocalization. In fact, confinement in a room as large as the home nursery room produced the same amount of vocalization as confinement in a small cage. We concluded that confinement was a factor only in that it prevented the puppy from returning to its familiar environment, and that the basic stimulus for eliciting this kind of distress vocalization was absence of the familiar.

On the practical side, we have adopted as a standard test situation for puppies 3 weeks of age and older a 2-ft cubical cage with wooden walls, a 1-in. wire mesh floor through which feces and urine can drop, and a 1-ft square opening in the top through which light can enter. Since such a box allows no visual contact with its surroundings (only olfactory ones), it should make little difference whether it is in the home pen or not. In fact, vocalization rates obtained in this cage are equally great whether it is placed in the home room of the puppy or in a strange room.

The only situation in which we have not obtained high vocalization rates was one in which we attempted to work with temperature changes. This involved placing the puppies in a virtually soundproof room, with sound absorbent walls, the only sound other than the puppies' vocalizations being that of a ventilating fan. Under these conditions isolated puppies would frequently go to sleep instead of vocalizing, suggesting that there is an alternative response to separation. Somewhat similar conditions, especially in the use of a ventilating fan providing a masking noise, were used by Fuller (1967) in his isolated experiments, in which he reported a relatively short-lived reaction to separation at 3 weeks. This phenomenon deserves further research.

Developmental Changes in the Separation Reaction

Elliot and Scott (1961) obtained vocalization counts from a large number of beagle puppies under two conditions each week from 3 through 12 weeks of age. In one condition, the puppy was placed alone and uncaged in his home room; in the other, the puppy was allowed to run freely in a strange room of similar size. In order to test for maturational as opposed to experiential changes, tests were initiated on different groups at 3, 6, 9 and 12 weeks. Later groups showed slightly higher initial rates but followed the same general curves as the earliest group, indicating that developmental changes were largely maturational.

Initial vocalization rates of puppies isolated in their home pen were moderately high at 3 weeks and declined slowly throughout subsequent ages. Initial rates in the strange room were much higher, rose rapidly to a plateau which was maintained through 8 weeks of age, and then dropped off rapidly.

A similar study with isolation in a strange pen was later done with cocker spaniels and extended for 4 additional weeks. The cocker rates were slightly higher but followed the same series of developmental changes. By 16 weeks the curve had very nearly approached zero.

It is obvious that the rate of distress vocalization in reaction to separation declines as puppies become older and more independent. This does not mean that they are not disturbed by separation but only that they no longer react primarily through vocalization. Separated adult dogs will also vocalize, but at much lower rates.

There are two changes associated with the beginning of the decline in distress vocalization. One is the fact that weaning from the breast is accomplished by most mothers by the time the puppies are 7 weeks old, although some bitches continue lactating longer. The other is the development of a new emotional reaction – fear of the strange – first apparent at approximately 7 weeks of age and growing stronger until it reaches a maximum state at 12 or 14 weeks (Scott, 1962). This emotional reaction might possibly have an inhibitory effect on vocalization. From an evolutionary viewpoint, vocalization would be less adaptive in an older animal, since the mother would be less likely to be available to respond and help. The developing fear reaction would then be the mechanism through which this change was effected. However, these are only speculative inferences.

Genetic Variation

While there are individual differences in rates of vocalization in reaction to separation, out of the several hundred puppies that we have observed and tested, we never found one that did not give this reaction in the standard test.

On the whole, breed differences tend to be slight. Most of the earlier work was done at different times with slight differences in technique. Our best data with breeds tested under comparable conditions comes from an experiment involving Shetland sheep dogs, Telomians, and F_1 hybrids between the two, with initial vocalization rates taken at 5 weeks of age. Despite the fact that the Telomians, a breed native to Malaysia where it is a common village dog in the camps of the aborigines, have been genetically isolated for several thousand years, their vocalization rates are not significantly different from those of the shelties (Fig. 2) and not strikingly different from beagles or cockers. The F_1 hybrids, however, show significantly higher rates than their sheltie mothers, another instance of hybrid vigor.

In an earlier experiment we sampled vocalization rates at morning and evening during 22-hr. daily separations in shelties and basenjis, the so-called African barkless dogs. These do show considerable differences, the basenji's rate being less than half that of the shelties (291 versus 689 per 10-min. session). The sheltie rate was considerably lower than the present data, probably because of a different experimental situation. None of the basenjis failed to show the reaction. We can conclude that the reaction of distress vocalization to separation is universal among dogs, and that this probably points to some sort of important survival function.

Adaptive Functions of Distress Vocalization

The most obvious function of this response in young puppies is that it serves as a call for help. A young puppy is so helpless and so vulnerable to predators that under wild conditions a lost or deserted puppy's survival must have depended upon its ability to attract the attention of its mother or other caretakers.

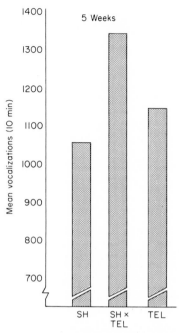

Fig. 2. Mean vocalization rates in a strange cage, comparing Shetland sheepdogs, Telomians, and F_1 hybrids of the two.

I have suggested elsewhere (Scott, 1967) that this emotional response also has an internal function. Separation produces an almost instantaneous vocalization response which, judging from the puppy's behavior, is accompanied by feelings of distress. These feelings are relieved almost immediately on reunion with familiar individuals and return to familiar places. From the viewpoint of reinforcement theory, repeated separation should result in learned motivation for contact with familiar individuals and places. Thus it can act as a major mechanism for the formation of social attachments. Once this motivation has been strongly established, it must contribute to allelomimetic behavior, since, in order to maintain continuous contact with other individuals, the puppy must perform the same activities. Allelomimetic behavior in turn has many adaptive functions in group life, being the essential basis of cooperative behavior in group-hunting, defense against predators, and so on. In any case, one of the strongest motivations of any dog is that for continuous social contact, either with other dogs or with its adopted human relatives. As Bacon and Stanley (1963) and Waller and Fuller (1961) have shown, this motivation has the properties of a general social drive.

Communicatory Function of Distress Vocalization

I have reviewed elsewhere (Scott, 1968) some of our experiments on the communicatory aspects of distress vocalization. One of the characteristics of such vocalization is its extraordinary variability in both the nature of the sounds and their loudness. Seen on the sonograph, distress vocalization induced by separation consists of a mixture of yelps, barks, whines, and other noises in no particular sequence or rhythm. This suggests the hypothesis that the sounds would be difficult to localize and thus give protection against predators in the same way that the variation in pitch and loudness of bird songs gives a ventriloqual effect to the human listener. However, when we tape-recorded such sounds and played them back with a speaker directed vertically, so as to give no directional effect, we found that human listeners, at any rate, had no difficulty localizing the direction from which the sounds came. Currently, our hypothesis is that the variation in sounds prevents auditory accommodation on the part of the listener, i.e., the noises produced by a young puppy are very different from the soothing sound of an electric fan.

Responsiveness of the mother to such sounds is difficult to determine except under special conditions. If the puppies are away from the mother and outside the home room, she becomes very responsive to their vocalizations, whether they are heard directly or played on a tape recorder. She vocalizes and attempts to get to the source of the sounds. On the other hand, the mother shows little reaction to the puppies vocalizing in the same room, other than to stay with them.

Maternal care in the dog is quite limited, consisting mostly of approaching the puppies, nosing and licking them (which stimulates defecation and urination), and allowing them to nurse. If the puppies are outside the usual nest area, she may pick them up and carry them back, although this is not done in every case. As they grow older, she may vomit food for them after being fed elsewhere and returning to them.

If a recording of the pup's vocalization is played to the mother while her pups are present, she may react simply by a quick inspection of the pups, apparently verifying the fact that they are silent, and pay no further attention. In short, the response to the signal of distress vocalization apparently depends on the interpretation of the situation by the mother and is not an automatic response, except in that the mother's attention is aroused, following which she investigates the situation. There is no evidence that the puppy's affect is transmitted directly to the mother.

We have also done certain unreported studies with vocalization and communication among adult dogs. One of the most common sounds produced by adult dogs is the bark — a short, sharp sound with consistent pitch and loudness. The bark is very easy to localize and carries over long distances. As observed in dogs living under seminatural conditions, barking seems to function as a warning signal, alerting any other dogs within hearing distance. In a group, barking by one individual is frequently taken up by others, raising the possibility of communication of affect. Barking also probably serves as a noxious stimulus on the listener, whether canine or of another species.

As observed in kennels, not all the dogs in a given area will bark. To elicit barking for recording purposes, we used the response of the dog to a person approaching or leaving its pen. The dog will bark fairly consistently; we incidentally found that barking occurred more commonly when the person was moving away from the dog than when he was approaching it. While transmission of information is involved, we have no evidence that affect is communicated directly. Groups of dogs will bark together, but this may be a common response to a single stimulus, rather than transmission of affect.

The vocal response of howling has much in common with the distress vocalization of puppies, since it most often occurs when a dog is alone. This reaction is difficult to elicit directly; and while sounds similar to howls, such as those produced by sirens and certain musical instruments, may occasionally induce howling, the only reliable eliciting stimulus is the sound of another dog howling. This in turn is most readily elicited by separating a dog from others – taking a mother's pups from her, for example. However, the response is by no means uniform. When separated, both dogs and wolves will sometimes howl back and forth to each other, and Pimlott (1960) has used this as a way of locating wolf packs and identifying individuals. A human cry simulating the howl of a wolf is very effective in arousing a howl in response (Theberge & Falls, 1967).

An interesting phenomenon is the chorus howling common to both dogs and wolves. One dog will start and others will quickly join, until the entire group is howling in unison. This pattern will occur when the dogs are not separated from each other, and offers a promising possibility for studying the communication of affect in dogs.

Conclusions

We have studied the development of two kinds of affect in young puppies. One of these, separation distress, has a clear communicatory function, although also it has other important functions. However, it does not appear to result in the communication of affect.

The developing fear reaction to the strange seems to reduce vocalization elicited by separation, although in older animals it may result in barking. Barking and howling seem to offer the most promising possibilities for the study of the communication of affect in dogs.

Development of Affect in Infant Rodents

Problems of Emotionality in Young Rodents

There are certain basic problems associated with emotionality in rodents in general, and young rodents in particular. The two typical measures of emotionality studied in the laboratory rat in an "open field" (which, in practice, is neither open nor a field, but a strange cage with an open top), are activity and defecation. The validity of these measures has not been verified nor even studied in a broad range of rodent species, and both measures are virtually impossible to obtain from young developing rodents before they emerge from the nest. Activity in the sense of exploratory behavior, which is in part a function of locomotor ability, may be largely absent in the neonatal rodent and changes rapidly as a function of development in later stages. Defecation in the young rodent occurs only in response to maternal stimulation. The absence of defecation by a young rodent in a novel environment therefore cannot be used as an indication of the absence of emotionality.

Basic Requirements for Development.

Rodent species having short gestation periods (20–30 days) give birth to young that are relatively immature. To survive they need maternal care. Certain temperatures, nutritional requirements, and physical stimulation are necessary for survival until the young are several weeks old. Maternal care usually supplies the developing young with these basic requirements, although some are supplied indirectly. Nests are built for other than parental reasons in some species, e.g., the house mouse and the golden hamster (Richards, 1967), and only prior to parturition in others, e.g., the laboratory rat (Lehrman, 1961). Regardless of when it is built, the nest serves, among other functions, as insulation for the pups. Other requirements are supplied directly by the mother. The lactating female's hovering, nursing, licking, and manipulation supply her litter with nutrition, warmth, and physical stimulation. Transporting and retrieving the young also supply physical stimulation. Nest cohabitants, whether they are littermates, older litters, the father, or miscellaneous conspecifics, may also supply some or all of these critical requirements.

In the Cairo spiny mouse (*Acomys cahirensis*) females help a mother during delivery, and even nurse the young (Dieterlen, 1962). The young of this species are rather well developed at birth: they are fully furred and have their eyes open. Howard (1949) found several instances where female deer mice, *Peromyscus maniculatus bairdii*, shared the nursing of litters in the field. Horner (1947) reported paternal care (retrieving, licking, crouching, and nest building) in male deer mice (*P. m. bairdii, P. m. gracilis, P. m. nebracensis, P. leucopus noveboracensis*).

The rodent pup's need for food is obvious. If nursing does not occur the litter will not survive. Hence it is a critical factor in development. The need for certain temperatures is less obvious. Anyone who has observed a lactating female rodent will recall that she spends considerable time with the pups but is not always nursing them. The young of most rodents have imperfect thermoregulatory systems at birth or have none at all. They are kept warm by the mother or other conspecifics. The nest serves as insulation to prevent the rapid loss of temperature when the mother is out of the nest for short periods of time. Grota and Ader (1969) found the median duration of time that the female rat spent away from her litter during the first week postpartum was 3 min. The internal body temperature of a 2-day-old rat pup can fall as much as 11°C during 30 min. if the mother is absent (Gelineo & Gelineo, 1952).

Physical stimulation of the young by the mother or some conspecific plays an important role in infant survival and development. Rats delivered by Caesarian sectioning and transferred to a germ-free incubator did not survive (Reyniers, 1953). Death was due to ruptured bladders and not to starvation. Tactile stimulation to the genital region is necessary for urination to occur.

Infantile stimulation has marked effects on growth and development. Although the results on the effects of infantile stimulation are by no means clear cut, moderate stimulation (e.g., handling) appears to accelerate eye opening, fur development, weight gain, learning ability, and brain development (Bernstein, 1952; Levine & Alpert, 1959; Levine, 1962).

During the course of development the female handles, licks, and grooms the young pups frequently. Since handling by an experimenter has profound effects on development, one could assume that maternal handling has similar effects on development.

Departures from the Optimal Environment

If for any reason, the optimal environment for development as just outlined is not present, then the infant rodent should be in a state of emotional arousal, resulting in increased activity, searching, and calling. These responses of the young should be within the limits of their developmental abilities. As responses, they can serve as signals to the mother for attention. Such care-soliciting or et-epimeletic behavior on the part of the young is a transfer of information from one individual (the pup) to another (the mother), and is clearly social in nature (Scott, 1956) and communicative in function.

Communication and Development of Abilities

Communication in young or neonatal rodents is primarily restricted to output with little input. So far as input is concerned, most rodents are born blind and deaf. In most small rodents, rats, mice, voles, hamsters, gerbils, etc., hearing develops during the second week of life. Several days to a week later, the eyes open. Olfaction is usually present at birth or within a few days after birth. Tactile abilities are fairly well developed at birth. Thus, during the first week of life, the only sensory input is touch and smell. It would be theoretically possible for the young to respond to certain alarm "pheromones" from the mother (if they exist) in response to some emotional situation such as the approach of a predator. However, there are no data to indicate this possibility.

The young of most rodent forms are capable of communicating information (output) at birth or within a few hours after birth. Zippelius and Schleidt (1956) have demonstrated that young rodents (*Apodemus flavicollis, Microtus arvalis,* and *Mus musculus*) emit ultrasonic calls when they are out of the nest. Such ultrasonic calls have been labeled "distress calls" or "desertion calls." However, we are aware of no reported research indicating that the neonate is indeed distressed when it is out of the nest. The assumption is that when the young are hungry, cold, or in a strange location they should be experiencing some degree of emotionality.

Both the communication of emotion and the reception of communicated information are limited in the young rodent by the developmental states of various physiological and motor systems. As the young develop, the opportunities for the expression and reception of affect signals expand.

Ultrasonic "Distress" Vocalization

Ultrasonic distress calls have been found in a wide variety of Murid and Cricetid rodents. Table 1 shows the various species whose young are known to emit ultrasonic calls when they are removed from the nest.

In a unique playback experiment, Allin and Banks (1971a) demonstrated that lactating females orient more directly toward recorded vocalizations of infant rats, even when no pup is present. Males and virgin females merely oriented toward the sound source.

Zippelius and Schleidt (1956) for field mice (*Apodemus flavicollis*), voles (*Microtus arvalis*), and house mice (*Mus musculus*), Noirot (1966) for non-inbred laboratory mice, *Mus musculus,* Noirot (1968) for the laboratory rat, *Rattus norvegicus,* and V. J. DeGhett (unpublished) with the Mongolian gerbil, *Meriones unguiculatus,* have shown an apparent relationship between eye opening and the disappearance of ultrasonic calling. Several factors could be responsible for this relationship. Eye opening is typically the last event to occur developmentally. With all of the sense modalities operating, there should be less uncertainty and possibly less cause for emotional arousal. As information from the environment increases, the degree of uncertainty and its associated emotionality should decrease (Simonov, 1969). Associated with the development of visual abilities is the development of locomotor coordination, which usually occurs a few days prior to eye opening. With visual and locomotor systems operating, coordinated and directional escape responses are possible, thus enabling the young to escape or avoid most emotionally arousing situations.

Temperature regulation also develops into its adult phase at about the time of eye opening. This is probably a major factor affecting the rate of distress calling. Young mice are poikilothermic until they are 7 days old (Lagerspetz, 1962). At this age there is an abrupt decline in the *intensity* and *duration* of ultrasonic

TABLE 1
Rodent Species in Which the Neonatal Young Emit Ultrasonic Calls

Species	Reference
Rattus norvegicus	Noirot (1968)
Rattus exulans	V. J. DeGhett & W. C. McCartney (unpublished)
Mus musculus	Zippelius & Schleidt (1956), Noirot (1966)
Mus minutoides	Sewell (1970)
Apodemus sylvaticus	Sewell (1970)
Apodemus flavicollis	Zippelius & Schleidt (1956)
Acomys caharinus	Sewell (1970)
Thamnomys sp.	Sewell (1970)
Praomys natalensis	Sewell (1970)
Peromyscus maniculatus bairdi	Hart & King (1966)
Peromyscus maniculatus gracilis	Hart & King (1966)
Peromyscus leucopus novaboricensis	V. J. DeGhett & W. C. McCartney (unpublished)
Mesocricetus auratus	Sewell (1970), E. Noirot, D. Pye, & M. Richards (unpublished)
Microtus arvalis	Zippelius & Schleidt (1956)
Microtus agrestis	Sewell (1970)
Clethrionomys glareolus	Sewell (1970)
Lagurus lagurus	Sewell (1970)
Meriones unguiculatus	Sewell (1970), DeGhett (unpublished)
Meriones libycus	Sewell (1970)
Gerbillus sp.	Sewell (1970)

calls, but *not* in the *rate* of calling (Noirot & Pye, 1969). Intensity and duration combined yield a measure of acoustic energy. In mice, the rate of calling drops to zero when the young are 13 days old, and their eyes are open (Noirot, 1966). From 7 to 13 days of age, the young are in a thermoregulatory transition stage. Day 13 corresponds to the beginning of the adult phase of temperature regulation, which is completely developed by Day 19 (Lagerspetz, 1962).

Laboratory rats achieve adult thermoregulation by about 21 days of age (Taylor, 1960). That the rate of ultrasonic calling in young rats is affected by ambient temperature has been aptly demonstrated by Allin and Banks (1971b). Low ambient temperatures (2 and 20°C) elicited higher rates of ultrasonic calling than did an approximation of the nest temperature (35°C) and a high temperature (40°C). Albino rats also emit more ultrasonic calls prior to eye opening than after eye opening (Noirot, 1968). Ultrasonic calls are occasionally heard after eye opening, but are absent by Day 21.

One very interesting characteristic of the rate of ultrasonic calling is the sharp increase and then decrease in the rate that seems to be related to unfolding of the external ears. This relationship has been found in laboratory rats, laboratory mice (Noirot, 1966, 1968) and Mongolian gerbils (DeGhett, unpublished).

Laboratory rats do not show evidence of hearing until 13 days of age (Bolles & Woods, 1964); mice show no evidence of auditory ability until 11 days of age (Williams & Scott, 1953); and Mongolian gerbils cannot hear until 15 days of age (DeGhett, 1969). All of these studies have used sonic or audible tones to test for hearing.

Noirot (1966) suggested that the rise in the rate of calling just before, and its subsequent decline after unfolding of the auditory pinnae might be due to an auditory feedback mechanism. She was unsuccessful in her attempts to prevent the ears from unfolding, so the possibility of feedback is still an open question. It is also possible that this developmental change in the rate of distress calling reflects some changing level of emotionality.

Work on rodent distress vocalization is relatively recent. That these calls are signals for maternal care now seems certain (Allin & Banks, 1972). The rate of calling seems to be affected by thermal stress at least in the albino rat (Allin & Banks, 1971). The extent to which hunger and strange locations affect the rate of calling is not yet known.

The "Jumpy Phase" in Mice

Williams and Scott (1953) and Fox (1965) reported the existence of a "jumpy phase" in the development of the mouse. According to Stewart (1968), who performed a genetic analysis of it, this phase is characterized by "violent episodes of running and jumping in response to seemingly inconsequential disturbances." Fox (1965) described the response as hypersensitivity, and Williams and Scott (1953) called it "flurries of wild escape."

The jumpy response can be triggered by a puff of air, movement of the cage, moderate noise, and tactile stimulation, and it appears to be contagious within the litter. It is first seen when the mouse pups are 10 to 14 days old and may last for 3 days in C57BL/6J mice and 12 or more days in DBA/2J mice (Stewart, 1968).

From its description, it appears to be an emotional response. Since the "jumpy phase" can be elicited by a broad variety of stimuli, it is possible that it could also be elicited by parental responses or signals. This scattering of the young might be an effective predatory defense mechanism. Little is known about the occurrence of this response in a variety of species. As a possible emotional response in infant mice, it warrants further investigation.

Emotionality in Young Rodents: Some Guidelines

It is unfortunate that more cannot be said concerning communication and affect in young rodents. That it cannot is due to the lack of data on infant emotionality. While adult rodents are popular research animals, young rodents are not, and studies on rodent development are uncommon. Greater emphasis must be placed on multivariate studies of rodent development across a variety of species. We need definitive studies of rodent development before truly meaningful manipulative experiments can be undertaken. As soon as the basic adaptations for early life are known, the functions of emotionality will be clearer. Most previous manipulative studies using young rodents have assessed the effects of such manipulations on adult life. Once we have clear descriptive data on early development, future research on infant emotionality should be directed toward gathering data on the immediate effects of manipulations in early life.

Discussion

Comparison of the Development of Affect in Dogs and Rodents

It is obvious from what we have said here that a great deal more is known about the development of affect in the dog than is known about most rodents. Until relatively recently, the existence of distress vocalization in young rodents remained undiscovered because of its ultrasonic quality, and the lack of any gross noticeable movements accompanying these calls. The only definite function that has so far been established in the rodents is a response to cold. There is some reason for believing that rodents may exhibit separation distress, since isolated adult male mice become progressively more irritable and show definite physiological changes. However, separation distress under conditions of comfortable temperatures has not been established in the infant rodents studied.

One of the major differences between distress vocalizations of the puppy and those of infant rodents is that the latter are ultrasonic. This immediately raises the problem of adaptive functions, particularly since the ultrasonic calls decrease as the animals grow older and markedly decrease at the time hearing appears. One hypothesis is that such calls would be inaudible to predators, but many predators including the dog are known to have auditory capacities well within the ultrasonic range. Cochlear potentials have been recorded from the coyote at 80 kHz., from the dog at 60 kHz., from the red fox at 65 kHz., and from the domestic cat at 100 kHz. to name a few (Peterson, Heaton, & Wruble, 1969). There is no information concerning the auditory sensitivity of the wolf, but its auditory range probably extends to at least 60 kHz. Even so, ultrasonic calls may be adaptive. Because they are highly directional and easily absorbed into the substrate, such as the next cavity or burrow, they should not carry any great distance. These facts should make it difficult for a predator to detect high-frequency calls made by young rodents in their normal environments.

The same characteristics would also make it difficult for the female rodent to discover the location of her separated young, but this may be compensated for by accompanying behavior patterns. When the young are out of the nest and vocalizing they are frequently turning or pivoting slowly in a circle. In effect the young rodent is emitting a highly directional beam while rotating in a circular fashion. Turning should maximize chances of this signal being intercepted by the mother. Regardless of the direction that the mother is moving or her location relative to the pup, she should intercept this signal and respond to it.

The Functions of Affect

In the past, the usual approach to the study of feeling states assumed them to be important chiefly as driving forces or as internally arising stimulation. In addition, one of the major functions of emotional responses is that they act as internal reinforcing mechanisms, and thus contribute to learned motivation of either a positive or negative nature. In another paper Scott (1969) pointed cut that an internal emotional response may also magnify and prolong the results of external stimulation. Simonov (1969) has hypothesized that emotions represent an emergency adaptive reaction, appearing in situations where there is a need to react, but insufficient information to give the organism a clear guide as to what response to make. Finally, as the results of our studies with separation distress show, the internal feeling state may activate behavior that has a signaling or communicatory function. Which of these diverse functions is important depends on the kind of emotional response that is involved, but it is likely that all functions are always present to some extent.

In the case of separation distress, all functions are apparent. As Waller and Fuller (1961) and Bacon and Stanley (1963) have shown, separated puppies act as if under the influence of a general social drive. The internal response to separation has the effect of prolonging the behavioral response to separation. Its internal reinforcing properties have great importance in attachment behavior and provide a motivational basis for allelomimetic behavior. Lastly, the young puppy's emotional state is directly related to vocalization, although it can also be inferred from changes in general activity, defecation, and urination rates (Elliot & Scott, 1961).

The Developmental Approach
to the Study of Affect and Communication

The developmental study of emotional responses gives us good insight to the function of emotional states, chiefly because we are able to observe changes in behavior as the capacities for emotional states appear. The young organism thus forms a sort of natural, albeit irreversible, experiment.

One of the most obvious facts about affect in infant animals is that it is, for the most part, directly related to communication. Infant animals have limited behavioral capacities, and the only way in which they can meet situations that require difficult adaptation is to signal for the help of other animals. For the most part, these signals have little or no effect on other infants. In dogs and many rodents, the infants are unable for a time even to hear the vocalizations of their littermates. Thus in the early stages there is no transmission of affect as there is in such phenomena as the "jumpy stage" in mice, in which one young mouse can presumably transmit his reactions to others by contact. This brings us to a consideration of communication of affect, which is perhaps best studied in human subjects, who are able to report their feeling states. In the following section, we shall suggest some of the directions in which this research might profitably proceed.

The Communication of Affect

Communication of a feeling state is not a necessary condition for producing an adaptive social response, but among humans, it is necessary for complete mutual understanding. Furthermore, a shared emotional response is a highly rewarding experience, and people constantly strive to achieve such experiences in various ways. In terms of the stimulus–response theory, the reception of an affect communicated by another is strongly reinforcing, and even more reinforcing if the communication is reciprocal.

To state this in more factual terms, the basis of all art and entertainment is the communication of affect. The final test of a painting, for example, is not the technical excellence of the artist's brushwork, but whether or not he is able to stimulate a strong feeling state.

More than this, people are constantly seeking shared emotional experiences, whether they be as simple as eating a good meal together or enjoying a cup of coffee or a beer in company, or whether they involve the complex and prolonged emotional experiences shared by the members of a dangerous arctic expedition. As William James long ago pointed out, one of the causes of war is the strong pleasure arising from shared emotional experiences.

All this suggests that the sharing of affect, which involves both input and output, is a major part of human experience. Whether or not it meets some basic biological or social need, it certainly forms one of the major pleasures of human experience, and we suggest that one of the more profitable directions in which the new science of communication could proceed is the exploration of the communication of affect. From our viewpoints, which are essentially genetic and developmental, we suggest that we begin with the hypothesis of differential capacities for transmitting and receiving affect, and that we assume that these two capacities are probably not correlated, but independent. Indeed, as we casually observe our fellow humans, we find that some of them are better transmitters of affect than others, as anyone can verify by watching a group of high school actors. Similarly, some individuals appear to be much more sensitive receivers than others. On the basis of general theory, we would expect there to be genetic variation in both capacities, modified by learning and training. In some limited research along these lines, the senior author once asked a group of college drama students to read what he thought was a moving piece of poetry as expressively as possible, in the hope of tape-recording a series of audible stimuli that could be used to test emotional receptiveness in others. As it happened, they had all been trained in the Stanislavski method, which requires that the actor try to imagine himself in a real situation which would call forth such an emotion, and then do what comes naturally. The most obvious result of the experiment was an extraordinary degree of individual variation in interpretation. It may very well be that there is no most effective single means of transmitting an emotion, but it is also possible that most people, even those who are reasonably skilled, do not know how they do it.

How is transmission effected? Most of the scientific work initiated by Darwin and followed up by Schlosberg (1952) and others used the method of asking actors to depict specific emotions through facial expressions, taking photographs, and asking subjects to name the emotion. The results were highly variable, no doubt partly due to the fact that in everyday life, transmissionis achieved through a combination of visual, auditory, and other sensory cues, and almost never in a static situation. It eventually became apparent that the chief problem with this method of experimentation lay in the verbal concepts of emotion held by the subjects (Block, 1957). That is, the chief process being studied was one of *naming* rather than transmission and reception. Other than these studies, the problem has been largely the concern of clinicians (Knapp, 1963), who have followed the line of discovering methods for better recognizing the emotional states signaled, but not directly revealed, by patients undergoing psychotherapy (Mahl, 1967). Again, this is a problem of recognition of signals rather than transmission of affect.

To look at the problem in another way, the writer's art is primarily one of transmitting various kinds of emotion effectively. It is a literary axiom that one of the poorest ways to do this is to describe the emotion felt by a fictitious person, and that it is far more effective to describe in detail the situation in which the character finds himself. Part of the situation is, of course, the behavior of the persons around him, and one of the hallmarks of a first-rate writer is that he is an excellent observer, perhaps better than most modern behavioral scientists.

We are not suggesting a scientific analysis of literature and art, although this could be a legitimate branch of the study of communication. Rather we suggest that the ways in which affect is communicated by artists and writers may give us hints for the analysis of a major communicatory process. As we have already stated, certain animal models, particularly barking and howling in the dog and wolf, have possibilities. Still another is based on the human–dog relationship. A man could make a systematic attempt to send affect, and its reception could be verified both by overt behavior and physiological measures in the dog.

As evidence for the importance of the phenomenon, we can only state the belief, based both on casual observation and on the fact that some form of entertainment plays an important part in every human society, that the sharing of affect is one of the great positive pleasures of human existence. As B. G. Rosenberg (private communication) has recently pointed out, a major defect of modern psychological science is the fact that it is based on a disease model and consequently neglects most of the positive aspects of living. The communication of affect is one avenue through which psychology can enter a new world of research.

References

Allin, J. T., & Banks, E. M. Effects of temperature on ultrasonic production by infant albino rats. *Developmental Psychobiology,* 1971, 4, 149–156.

Allin, J. T., & Banks, E. M. Functional aspects of ultrasonic production by infant albino rats. *Animal Behaviour,* 1972, in press.

Bacon, W. E., & Stanley, W. C. Effect of a deprivation level in puppies on performance maintained by a passive person reinforcer. *Journal of Comparative Physiological Psychology,* 1963, 56, 783–785.

Bacon, W. E., & Stanley, W. C. Reversal learning in neonatal dogs. *Journal of Comparative & Physiological Psychology,* 1970, 70, 344–350.

Bernstein, L. A note on Christie's "Experimental naivete and experiential naivete." *Psychological Bulletin,* 1952, 49, 38–40.

Block, J. Studies in the phenomenology of emotions. *Journal of Abnormal & Social Psychology,* 1957, 54, 358–363.

Bolles, R. C., & Woods, P. J. The ontogeny of behaviour in the albino rat. *Animal Behaviour,* 1964, 12, 427–441.

DeGhett, V. J. Behavioral development of the Mongolian gerbil (*Meriones unguiculatus*). *American Zoologist,* 1969, 9, 568. (Abstract)

DeGhett, V. J., Stewart, J. M., & Scott, J. P. Habituation of distress vocalization response of puppies of different dog breeds in constant and varying environments. *American Zoologist,* 1970, 10, 294.

Dieterlen, F. Geburt und Geburtshilfe bei der Stachelmaus, *Acomys cahirinus. Zeitschrift fur Tierpsychologie,* 1962, 19, 191–222.

Elliot, O., & Scott, J. P. The development of emotional distress reactions in puppies. *Journal of Genetic Psychology,* 1961, 99, 3–22.

Fox, M. W. Reflex ontogeny and behavioural development of the mouse. *Animal Behaviour,* 1965, 13, 234–241.

Fredericson, E. Distributed versus massed experience in a traumatic situation. *Journal of Abnormal & Social Psychology,* 1950, 45, 259–266.

Fuller, J. L. Experiential deprivation and later behavior. *Science,* 1967, 158, 1645–1652.

Gelineo, S., & Gelineo, A. La temperature du nid du rat et sa signification biologique. *Bulletin Academie Serbe Science,* 1952, 4, 197–210.

Grota, L. J., & Ader, R. Continuous recording of maternal behaviour in *Rattus norvegicus. Animal Behaviour,* 1969, 17, 722–729.

Hart, F. M., & King, J. A., Distress vocalizations of young in two subspecies of *Peromyscus maniculatus. Journal of Mammalogy*, 1966, 47, 287–293.

Horner, E. B. Paternal care of young mice of the genus *Peromyscus. Journal of Mammalogy*, 1947, 28, 31–36.

Howard, W. E. Dispersal, amount of inbreeding, and longevity in a local population of prairie deermice on the George Reserve, Southern Michigan. *Contributions to the Laboratory of Vertebrate Biology, University of Michigan*, 1949, 43, 1–52.

Knapp, P. H. (Ed.) *Expression of the emotions in man.* New York: International Univ. Press, 1963.

Lagerspetz, K. The postnatal development of homoiothermy and cold resistance in mice. *Experientia*, 1962, 18, 282–284.

Lehrman, D. S. Hormonal regulation of parental behavior in birds and infrahuman mammals. In W. C. Young (Ed.), *Sex and internal secretions.* Vol. 2 (3rd ed.). Baltimore: Williams & Wilkins, 1961.

Levine, S. Psychophysiological effects of infantile stimulation. In E. L. Bliss (Ed.), *Roots of behavior.* New York: Harper, 1962.

Levine, S., & Alpert, M. Differential maturation of the central nervous system as a function of early experience. *Archives of General Psychiatry*, 1959, 1, 403–405.

Mahl, G. F. Some clinical observations on nonverbal behavior in interviews. *Journal of Nervous & Mental Disease*, 1967, 144, 492–505.

Noirot, E. Ultra-sounds in young rodents. I. Changes with age in albino mice. *Animal Behaviour*, 1966, 14, 459–462.

Noirot, E. Ultra-sounds in young rodents. II. Changes with age in albino rats. *Animal Behaviour*, 1968, 16, 129–134.

Noirot, E., & Pye, D. Sound analysis of ultrasonic distress calls of mouse pups as a function of their age. *Animal Behaviour*, 1969, 17, 340–349.

Olds, J. Self-stimulation of the brain. *Science*, 1958, 127, 315–323.

Peterson, E. A., Heaton, W. C., & Wruble, S. D. Levels of auditory response in fissiped carnivores. *Journal of Mammalogy*, 1969, 50, 566–578.

Pimlott, D. H. The use of tape-recorded howls to locate timber wolves. 22nd Midwest Fish and Wildlife Conference. Toronto, 1960.

Plotnik, R., & Delgado, J. M. R. Aggression and pain in unrestrained rhesus monkeys. In B. E. Eleftheriou & J. P. Scott (Eds.), *The physiology of aggression and defeat.* New York: Plenum, 1971.

Reyniers, J. A. Germ-free life. *Lancet*, 1953, 933–934.

Richards, M. P. M. Maternal behaviour in rodents and lagomorphs. In A. McLaren (Ed.), *Advances in Reproductive Physiology*, Vol. 2. New York: Academic Press, 1967.

Schlosberg, H. The description of facial expressions in terms of two dimensions. *Journal of Experimental Psychology*, 1952, 44, 227–237.

Scott, J. P. The analysis of social organization in animals. *Ecology*, 1956, 37, 213–221.

Scott, J. P. Critical periods in the development of social behavior in puppies. *Psychosomatic Medicine*, 1958, 20, 42–54.

Scott, J. P. Critical periods in behavioral development. *Science*, 1962, 138, 949–958.

Scott, J. P. The development of social motivation. In D. Levine (Ed.), *Nebraska symposium on motivation.* Lincoln, Nebraska: Univ. of Nebraska Press, 1967.

Scott, J. P. Observation. In T. A. Sebeok (Ed.), *Animal communication.* Bloomington, Indiana: Indiana Univ. Press, 1968.

Scott, J. P. The emotional basis of social behavior. *Annals of the New York Academy of Sciences*, 1969, 159, 777–790.

Scott, J. P., & Bronson, F. H. Experimental exploration of the et-epimeletic or care-soliciting behavioral system. In P. H. Leiderman & D. Shapiro (Eds.), *Psychobiological approaches to social behavior.* Stanford, California: Stanford Univ. Press, 1964.

Scott, J. P., & Fuller, J. L. *Genetics and the social behavior of the dog.* Chicago, Illinois: Univ. of Chicago Press, 1965.

Sewell, G. D. Ultrasonic signals from rodents. *Ultrasonics*, 1970, 8, 26–30.

Simonov, P. V. Studies of emotional behavior of humans and animals by Soviet psychologists. *Annals of the New York Academy of Sciences,* 1969, **159**, 1112–1121.

Stewart, J. M. Genetic and non-genetic determinants of the jumpy phase in the development of *Mus musculus. American Zoologist,* 1968, **8,** 4. (Abstract No. 65).

Stewart, J. M., De Ghett, V. J., & Scott, J. P. Age of onset of puppies' distress vocalizations in strange and familiar situations. *American Zoologist*, 1970, **10**, 293.

Taylor, P. M. Oxygen consumption in newborn rats. *Journal of Physiology*, 1960, **154**, 153–168.

Theberge, J. B., & Falls, J. B. Howling as a means of communication in timber wolves. *American Zoologist*, 1967, **7**, 331–338.

Waller, M. B., & Fuller, J. L. Preliminary observations on early experience as related to social behavior. *American Journal of Orthopsychiatry*, 1961, **31**, 254–266.

Williams, E., & Scott, J. P. The development of social behavior patterns in the mouse, in relation to natural periods. *Behaviour*, 1953, **6**, 35–64.

Zippelius, H. M., & Schleidt, W. M. Ultraschall-laute bei jungen Mausen. *Naturwissenschaften*, 1956, **43**, 502.

AUTHOR INDEX

Numbers in italics refer to the pages on which the complete references are listed.

A

Ader, R., 140, *148*
Ainsworth, M. D., 25, 26, 27, 29, 39, *44*
Ainsworth, M. D. S., 23, 24, 25, 26, 27, 37,
    38, 39, 40, 41, *44*
Allin, J. T., 141, 142, 143, *148*
Alpert, M., 140, *149*
Alpert, R., 24, 26, *48*
Amatruda, C. S., 39, *45*
Ambrose, J. A., 35, 39, *44*
Ames, L. B., 39, *45*

B

Bacon, W. E., 132, 136, 145, *148*
Baer, D. M., 24, *46, 47*
Bandura, A., 58, *65*
Banks, E. M., 141, 142, 143, *148*
Bartlett, R. C., 110, 113, *117*
Bayley, N., 39, *44*
Beller, E. K., 22, 23, 24, 25, 26, 30, 31, *44*
Bellugi, U., 92, *96*
Berlyne, D. E., 97, 100, 101, 102, 103, 104,
    105, 110, 112, 113, *117*
Bernstein, L., 140, *148*
Block, J., 147, *148*
Bolles, R. C., 143, *148*
Boudewijns, W. J. A., 104, *117*
Bowlby, J., 22, 23, 24, 25, 26, 27, 37, *44,
45*
Brackbill, Y., 35, *45*
Braine, M. D. S., 76, *96*
Brown, R., 92, *96*
Bühler, C., 39, *45*
Buss, A. H., 120, *128*

C

Cairns, R. B., 23, 24, 25, 27, 37, *45*
Caldwell, B. M., 23, 26, *45*
Casterline, D., 79, 85, *96*
Castner, B. M., 39, *45*
Cattell, P., 39, *45*
Cazden, C., 92, *96*
Chasdi, E. H., 22, 23, 24, 25, 26, 30, *48*
Chomsky, N., 69, *96*
Cohen, J. C., 22, 23, 24, 25, 26, 30, *48*
Croneberg, C. G., 79, 85, *96*
Crozier, J. B., 103, *117*

D

Day, H. I., 103, *117*
DeGhett, V. J., 132, 143, *148, 150*
Delgado, J. M. R., 130, *149*
Dieterlen, F., 139, *148*
Drake, P. F., 111, *117*
Durbin, M., 58, *65*

E

Elliot, O., 134, 145, *148*
Emerson, P. E., 25, 26, 29, 35, 36, 39, 40,
    48
Erikson, E. H., 4, *18*
Etzel, B. C., 35, *45*
Evans, D. R., 103, *117*

F

Faigin, H., 22, 23, 24, 25, 26, 30, *48*

Falls, J. B., 138, *150*
Fechner, G. T., 100, 101, *117*
Fleener, D. E., 25, *45*
Fox, M. W., 143, *148*
Frank, H., 110, *117*
Fredericson, E., 132, *148*
Freud, S., 22, *45*
Fuller, J. L., 130, 131, 134, 136, 145, *148,*
    150
Furchner, C. S., 2, *18*

G

Galanter, E., 22, *47*
Gallimore, R., 32, *45*
Gardner, A. R., 74, 75, *96*
Gardner, B. T., 74, 75, *96*
Gelb, I., 64, *65*
Gelineo, A., 140, *148*
Gelineo, S., 140, *148*
Gesell, A., 39, 40, 41, *45, 46*
Gewirtz, H. B., 35, 36, 37, 41, *46, 47*
Gewirtz, J. L., 20, 22, 23, 24, 25, 26, 28,
    29, 30, 31, 32, 33, 34, 35, 36, 37, 38,
    39, 41, *46, 47*
Gibb, C. A., 120, *128*
Gilliland, A. R., 39, *47*
Goodall, J., 52, *65*
Griffiths, R., 39, *47*
Grota, L. J., 140, *148*
Gunderson, K., 120, *128*

H

Halverson, H. M., 39, *45*
Harlow, H. F., 2, *18,* 22, 25, *47*
Harlow, M., 22, *47*
Hart, F. M., 142, *149*
Hartup, W. W., 30, *47*
Hayes, C., 74, *96*
Hayes, K. J., 74, *96*
Heathers, G., 23, *47*
Heaton, W. C., 144, *149*
Hewes, G. W., *65*
Hockett, C. F., 54, *65*
Honig, A. S., 23, 26, *45*
Horner, E. B., 139, *149*
Howard, W. E., 139, *149*

I

Ilg, F. L., 39, *45*
Inhelder, B., 59, *65*

K

Kellogg, L. A., 74, *96*
Kellogg, W. N., 74, *96*
Kemp, B., 32, *45*
Kessen, W., 103, *117*
King, J. A., 142, *149*
Klima, E. S., *96*
Knapp, P. H., 147, *149*
Köhler, W., 52, *65*

L

Lagerspetz, K., 141, 142, *149*
Landau, R., 34, *47*
Lawrence, M. S., 22, 23, 24, 25, 26, 30, *48*
Lehrman, D. S., 139, *149*
Levin, H., 23, *48*
Levine, S., 140, *149*
Levy, D. M., 39, *47*
Lewis, M., 24, 25, *45*
Lieberman, P. H., 74, *96*
Lorenz, K., 22, *47*
Lubbock, J., 57, *65*

M

McClelland, W. A., 120, *128*
McConville, C. B., 120, *128*
McDonnell, P., 105, *117*
McDougall, W., 22, *47*
McKee, J. P., 22, 23, 24, 25, 26, 30, *48*
Maccoby, E. E., 23, 29, 30, 34, *47, 48*
Mahl, G. F., 147, *149*
Masters, J. C., 29, 30, 34, *47*
Miller, G. A., 22, *47*
Misbach, L. E., 105, *117*
Munsinger, H., 103, *117*
Myers, A. E., 120, *128*

N

Nicki, R. M., 105, *117*
Noirot, E., 141, 142, 143, *149*
Nowlis, V., 22, 23, 24, 25, 26, 30, *48*

O

Ogden, C. K., 99, *118*
Olds, J., 130, *149*

P

Parham, L. C. C., 102, 105, *117*
Peterson, E. A., 144, *149*
Piaget, J., 22, *47*, 59, *65*
Pimlott, D. H., 138, *149*
Plotnik, R., 130, *149*
Premack, D., 53, 54, 56, *65*, 75, 77, *96*
Pribram, K. H., 22, *47*
Pye, D., 142, *149*

R

Rau, L., 24, 26, *48*
Reyniers, J. A., 140, *149*
Reynolds, F., 52, *65*
Reynolds, V., 52, *65*
Rheingold, H. L., 35, *47*
Richards, I. A., 99, *118*
Richards, M. P. M., 139, *149*
Rosenblum, L. A., 13, *18*
Rosenthal, M. K., 24, *47, 48*
Ross, H. W., 35, *47*
Rostow, W., 99, *118*

S

Sackett, G. P., 1, *18, 25, 48*
Salzen, E. A., 22, *48*
Schaffer, H. R., 25, 26, 29, 35, 36, 39, 40, *48*
Schleidt, W. M., 141, 142, *150*
Schlosberg, H., 147, *149*
Schönpflug, W., 105, *118*
Scott, J. P., 22, 23, *48*, 130, 131, 132, 134, 135, 136, 140, 143, 145, *148, 149, 150*
Sears, P. S., 22, 23, 24, 25, 26, 30, *48*
Sears, R. R., 22, 23, 24, 25, 26, 30, 37, *48*
Sewell, G. D., 142, *150*
Shaffer, L. F., 22, *48*
Shirley, M. M., 39, *48*
Simonov, P. V., 141, 145, *150*
Siple, P., *96*

Slobin, D. I., 92, *96*
Sluckin, W., 22, *48*
Spalding, D. A., 22, *48*
Spitz, R. A., 39, *48*
Stanley, W. C., 132, 136, 145, *148*
Stewart, J. M., 132, 143, *148, 150*
Stingle, K. C., 23, 33, *47*
Stokoe, W. C., 79, 85, *96*

T

Tannenbaum, J., 23, 26, *45*
Taylor, P. M., 142, *150*
Tharp, R. G., 32, *45*
Theberge, J. B., 138, *150*
Thompson, H., 39, 40, 41, *45, 46*
Tolstoi, L. N., 99, *118*

V

Vitz, P. C., 106, *118*

W

Waller, M. B., 136, 145, *150*
Washburn, R. W., 39, *48*
Weisberg, P., 35, *48*
Wescott, R., 58, *65*
Whiting, J. W. M., 22, 23, 24, 25, 26, 30, *48, 49*
Williams, E., 143, *150*
Wittig, B. A., 25, *44*
Wolf, K. M., 39, *48*
Woods, P. J., 143, *148*
Wright, C. M., 23, 26, *45*
Wruble, S. D., 144, *149*

Y

Yarrow, L. J., 25, 26, 38, 39, 40, 41, *49*

Z

Zimmermann, R. R., 22, 25, *47*
Zippelius, H. M., 141, 142, *150*

SUBJECT INDEX

A

Aesthetics, 97-118, 146
  hedonic response, 101
  role of complexifying, 102-115
    of interestingness in, 97-118
    of novelty in, 102-115
    of pleasantness in, 97-118
Affect
  communication of, 99, 146-148
  functions of, 145
Affection, 2, 7
Association, *see* Completion, Imitation
Attachment, 2-3, 19-24, 26, 36, 39, 42
  "affectional tie," 22
  contact comfort, 2-3
  infant-mother bond, 3
  particular person, 20
  primary social relationship, 22
  response, 24
  S-R index, 34
  summarizing variables, 36
Avoidance, 42

C

Case-history method, 99
Chimpanzee, language in, 53, 58, 74-77
Cognition, 51, 53
Completion, 61-62, *see also* Imitation
Consonant, 71
Culture, 52-53
Curiosity, 5, 8

D

Dependence, 19-20, 24, 26, 34, 36, 39, 42
  class of persons, 20

direct positive control, 26
limiting conditions, 26
response, 24
S-R index, 34
summarizing variables, 36
Development, 40, 130-131
  levels of, 130-131
  stages of, 130-131
Dogs, 130-138, 144-145
  barking, 137-138
  howling, 138

E

Echolalia, 60-61
Emotion, 3, 4, 29
  open-field, 4
  responses to, 29
Exploration, 6, 102-115

F

Fear stimulus, 5
Fixed action patterns, 16

G

Gestalt psychology, 98, 103

H

Human infant, 3

I

Icon, 58-65

154

Imitation, 58, 60-62, *see also* Completion
  in autistic children, 60-61
  mental image as, 58-59
Individual differences, 31

L

Language, 4, 12, 53-56, 59, 63-64, 68-70,
  72, 74-96
  acquisition of, 72, 75-77, 91-96
  ambiguity of in linguistic symbolism, 70
  in chimpanzees, 53-56, 74-77
  in deaf, 78-96
  displacement in, 55
  English, 70, 78-79, 90
  iconic aspects of, 59
  of lust, 12
  polysemous character of, 65
  relation of to symbolization, 51, 58
  and structure of linguistic symbolism,
    68-70
  visual-gestural, 63-64, 75-77, 90
  vocal-oral, 63-64, 68, 77
Love, 2, 6, 7

M

Machines, affective communication with,
  119-128
Manners, 5
Memory, 51, 63-64, 90-91
  in deaf, 90-91
Morpheme, 70-71
Motherhood, 3, 6, 30
  ambivalent maternal stage, 3
  maternal condition, 6
Music, 104-110

O

Overgeneralization, 93-96

P

Phoneme, 53-65, 68, 71
Play, 9-11
Poetry, 111-115
Psychoanalysis, 98
Punishment, 8, 119-128

R

"Relevance" in psychology, 116
Respresentation, *see* Symbolization
Rodents, 138-145

S

Scaling theory, 100
Security, 4
Semantic differential, 102-103, 111-114
Sentence, 53, 71-74
  complex propositional phrase, 72-73
  simple propositional phrase, 72
Separation distress, 36, 132-135
Sexual behavior, 13, 16
Socialization, 30
Symbolization, 51, 53, 56-58, 63
  in chimpanzee, 53-58
  in dogs, 56-58
Syntax, 69, 71-72, 78
  ambiguity in, 69
  constraints in, 72-74
  in language of deaf, 95

V

Vowel(s), 71

W

Word(s), 53, 68, 70-71, 73
Writing systems, 64